The Good, the Bad & the Boozy

CHRIS MARSH

by
Chris Marsh & Chris Smith

INTRODUCTION

On writing this book, I hope that younger players can read and learn from the mistakes that I have made. I grew up in the "Booze Culture" but for the good of the game, that has now almost disappeared. Dedication and hard work could now make a talented youngster a millionaire, not bad for someone who, like myself, might have hardly any qualifications.

When asked to do this book, I made a conscious decision not to mention the names of my team-mates in any compromising stories - not that they are guilty, but I just wanted to get my story across without the need for getting anyone in trouble!

I have made some great friends over the years, and I will always look back at my time with my team-mates with great pleasure because I love them all.

I would like to thank Chris Smith and Steve Rushton for their help with the book, and I would like to say sorry to the people who, through drink, I have unintentionally hurt. I am a private person, and wish that my private life stay that way, but the people near to me, who I love, know who they are especially my Mum, Dad and brothers - this is for you.
I would like to dedicate this book to the most important beautiful girl in my life, my daughter Harriet - I love you xxx.

The Good, the Bad & the Boozy

Chris Marsh

WHO ARE YOU?

Chris Marsh may not be a household name, but in the Black Country he is something of a legend for his antics both on and off the football pitch. He played for Walsall, Wycombe Wanderers and Northampton Town and it's fair to say his notoriety for having a good time was a constant companion as he carved a reputation as a loveable rascal who could also play a bit.

His trademark step-over was acclaimed at Walsall where he was hugely popular with the fans, especially those he met in the bar afterwards. His popularity peaked when he wrote a hugely entertaining weekly newspaper column taking the mickey out of his Walsall team mates.

In his prime he became a transfer target for Liverpool but an ill-timed injury wrecked a possible dream move and that sent him on a downward spiral into the depths of alcoholism that eventually wrecked his marriage.

This book is Chris's warts-and-all account of his career. It aims to provide both an amusing insight into the real world of a lower league professional footballer in comparison with his millionaire peers in the money-laden Premiership, and at the same time provide a stark warning to those taking the first steps in football.

Yes, football can be extremely lucrative, but he wants those setting out to beware the pitfalls that can lie ahead - especially the demon drink. From the WAGS to the parasite hangers-on there are many temptations and it is all too easy to give in.

Basically his message is to stay fit and healthy, enjoy your life to the full but at the same time apply yourself 100 per cent to your profession. The rewards will come later.

BECKHAM AND ME

I'd never been a Manchester United fan, that was until January 24, 1998. That was the biggest day in my football career, and arguably the biggest in Walsall Football Club's history too.

For that was the day we played Manchester United at Old Trafford in the fourth round of the FA Cup in front of a full house of 54,669 and I can tell you it still sends tingles down my spine when I think about it. And little was I to know that 24 hours after the game something would happen which made headlines all over the world.

We went to Manchester on the Friday for a tour of the ground and we were treated like royalty. Alex Ferguson greeted us personally and made us feel welcome which was a nice gesture. The manager of the biggest club in the world taking the time to shake hands with each and every one of us really made me feel quite humble yet proud at the same time.

It was during the look around that the United kit manager told us it was club policy that the team would not swap shirts after the game which was a great shame. Still that saved us from taking part in an undignified scramble because it would have been embarrassing when the referee blew the final whistle if there were 11 of us standing in a circle around David Beckham trying to get his shirt!

As we were in the the tunnel just before we went out I told Becks that I knew we couldn't swap shirts, but if there was anything he could get me as a memento of the day I would be grateful. He said he would see what he could do and I thought to myself: Yeah right, a world superstar is really going to put himself out for me. I'll bet that's what he says to every player just to get them to leave him alone.

It was at that moment that I actually began to appreciate just what intense pressure he must be under all the time. He is living his life in a goldfish bowl and his every move is scrutinised in the media. I'll bet there were a number of occasions when he must have wanted to lash out, especially to an intrusive photographer, but I can't remember him ever blowing a gasket. He has always managed to retain his dignity no matter what has been thrown at him and that must be extremely difficult. I don't know if I could keep things under control if I ever found myself in a position like that.

Anyway we took to the pitch with the most amazing team talk from manager Jan Sorensen still in our thoughts. It was absolutely bizarre. Here we were, taking on the top team in the country packed with megastars and galacticos on their own muckheap and Jan had told us: Forget who you're playing, forget their reputation, they're no better than you.

Andy Cole, David Beckham, Gary Neville, Ole Gunnar Solskjaer they're all crap. Hear me? They're shit. We're on a great run and they will be crapping themselves in there. Reputations count for nothing in the Cup and they're afraid of us because they know we are as good as they are on our day. Just think of the headlines if we beat them. It will be the biggest shock ever in the history of the FA Cup so let's go and give it our best shot.

Now I could appreciate him trying to psyche us up and give us a lift, but I must admit I found it hard not to laugh out loud when he said Beckham was shit. I really think Jan went a bit overboard there!

We emerged from the tunnel and the scenes that greeted us literally took my breath away. The ground was not recognisable from the empty shell we had seen a few hours earlier and it was a seething cauldron, full of passion, and the noise was deafening. I don't know about Beckham being shit, but there was certainly a strange feeling in the pit of my stomach and at the time I wondered if I'd get through 45 minutes without urgent need of the toilet!

United's players are used to such crowds and such occasions, but for us oiks out of the sticks it was an unbelievable experience and something I have never encountered since. What made it especially memorable for us players was that 8,500 Walsall fans had made the journey and believe me, they really made some noise. When you consider that is pretty well double the number of fans who used to turn up for home games at Bescot, you can appreciate just what it meant to them and us.

They were in full voice right from the word go and sang themselves hoarse through the entire game. They were an absolute credit to the club and I'm sure they, like me, have vivid memories of Old Trafford.

Anyway there were no miracles, no upsets and United duly spanked us 5-1 which was about the right result. We had been chasing shadows virtually all game and we were already 5-0 when Roger Boli scrambled home our consolation goal. In the very unlikely scenario that we did score, we had all agreed to do a mock faint, this was an idea of John Hodge, who had kept constantly reminding us of this if the unthinkable happened. Well, when it did, we all obliged by falling to the ground, much to the delight of the Old Trafford crowd - but unfortunately the architect of this idea was too busy hugging and kissing the goalscorer to notice! But that goal in itself was some form of meagre reward because there was not one single Walsall player who didn't run his bollocks off that day and the fact that we got a standing ovation from the United fans speaks volumes for the effort we put in.

We did ourselves proud, the fans and especially Walsall FC because we made over £500,000 which for a club the size of Walsall was an absolute Godsend. I can still see the twinkle in the eye of the club owner Jeff Bonser - but I know he will have been disappointed not to get a draw to take them back to Bescot for a replay - and more cash!

In the players bar afterwards Beckham took the trouble to track me down - he didn't have to look too far - and apologised for not being able to get me a shirt. He said he had asked as a one-off occasion because it had been such a great day out for us, but the club couldn't change their policy.

It was good of him to have made the effort though. I thanked him and said thanks for trying anyway and with that he took me up to the bar and bought me a drink. I was hoping somebody would take a picture of it for posterity - the legend having a drink at Old Trafford and Beckham was there too!

He told me to make sure I bought the Sunday papers next day because he was going to be front page news. Bloody hell I thought. What could it be? Had I played that well he was going to hang up his boots? Was he retiring? Was he being transferred? Had he stuck one on Fergie? All sorts of bizarre ideas came rushing into my head.

What is it, I asked. I couldn't contain myself. He said he couldn't dare tell me yet, but admitted that something was going to dominate the front pages next day.

It turned out that he had asked Victoria to marry him and she had said yes. Some of the United players did not even know yet so that is why he just couldn't let on. I could see from his face that he was desperate to tell someone because he was obviously proud and chuffed at the same time, but you can understand why he had to keep his secret for a few more hours.

Just imagine the killing I could have made at the bookies if he had let me in on his secret. Marshy with a world exclusive - I wouldn't have been able to get to a betting shop quickly enough!

I was so happy that not only had he come looking for me, but that he had actually put himself out to try and get me something and had almost let me into a secret that would rock the world. In my book Becks is a top man and I will not have a word said against him. Okay he is permanently in the spotlight and not just for his football, but face to face he is just an ordinary down-to-earth bloke and I couldn't believe how humble he really is.

The same applies for Alex Fergusson. People have their own views of him and some players have been on the wrong end of the notorious "hair drier" treatment in the dressing rooms, but what I witnessed was a really down to earth bloke just like Becks and he actually told Jan Sorensen that he deserved a massive pay rise for what he had achieved at such a small club.

He can come across as a surly, aggressive boss who lets his players know exactly where they stand and what he expects from them, but I am sure he does it for a reason. After all, being manager of one of the biggest clubs in the world for 20 years with a staggering success rate is a truly amazing achievement so he must be doing something right!

The one thing that annoyed us as players after the game though, was that one of our own local reporters slagged us off in his match report, saying we were second best, looked out of our depth and the defenders could have marked their opponents better. The fact that we had lost to one of the top teams in the world at the time seemed to have escaped this idiot completely and he went down in all the players' estimations after that.

There was just one more little incident that occurred as we were leaving the stadium and for me it sums up the chasm between Premiership superstars and lower league players. As we headed out into the night sky towards the coach it seemed there were a million fireworks being let off, but in fact it was newspaper photographers and fans taking pictures of the players as they trooped out. I was just behind Solskjaer and I was temporarily blinded as it seemed a million flashbulbs were going off at the same time. He paused politely for a few seconds, smiled obligingly and yet as soon as he moved away and I appeared in the doorway, the night was pitch black again.

I had said farewell to Becks, given him a hug like best buddies and wished him all the best for the World Cup. And what happened? He got sent off against Argentina and it seemed the whole world had turned against him. He and his family received death threats, evil chants about his wife cropped up around the country and all of a sudden he was public enemy No 1. That's what happens when you become mates with 'lucky Marshy'. Well I wish I could call him a mate anyway!

DEAD MAN WALKING

I'm not averse to the odd pint or two and so for me, a pre-season tour to Dublin was like putting Dracula in charge of a bloodbank.

I hadn't long been with Wycombe Wanderers and spending three days in Ireland was the perfect preparation for the new season - and of course it helped the lads bond, especially the new kids on the block like me. After all, I had something of a reputation to live up to and had to set down the benchmark for all those who wanted to try and keep up with me.

The gaffer Lawrie Sanchez treated us as grown-ups and didn't mind us going out to have the odd drink on condition that we put the work in next day and that's exactly what we did. We trained really hard and, in Gazza's words, refuelled suitably. Well, when you're in Dublin, you've got to haven't you? If you don't like the Guinness there then there's no hope for you.

Little did I know that there was a dress code for nights out on the town - but I soon found that out when I went to the hotel lobby for the 6pm meet-up. The rest of the lads were there in smart casual while I had on jeans and white trainers, which evidently was a big no-no and I was told that unless I changed my shoes I couldn't go out with them. A night on the piss without 'the Legend' was just unthinkable. Something had to be done.

9

At that time of day all the shops were shut and nobody had a spare pair of shoes that would be suitable. One of the directors thought he had the solution and told me to follow him to his room because he had a spare pair.

He did have some all right, but they were the most horrible, grotesque pair of cream tan slip-ons you could possibly imagine. They were horrendous and I wouldn't be seen dead in them. Not wishing to hurt his feelings (and you don't want to cross the directors when you're new to a club) I thanked him very much but said they did not quite fit properly and didn't want to run the risk of picking up a silly injury by wearing shoes that were not quite right. He said I was right of course, we didn't want any risks, and somehow I just about managed to keep a straight face. I really would have been a laughing stock wearing them.

I thought to myself: That's it, there's no way I'm going out on the piss tonight Marshy old son, but I hadn't reckoned on the determination of the other players who wanted to see the Legend strut his stuff in the bars. They took me to the hotel lost property office and we encountered a bloke in a black suit who looked like a genuine Irish navvy - a huge geezer built like a brick shithouse and with an accent to match.

Shit, I don't fancy my chances with him if I get back pissed, I thought. But anyway he was as nice as pie and before you could say begorrah Mick - no idea if that was his name but it is now! - he came up trumps and like a magician produced a cracking pair of shoes from out of nowhere.

By now I was desperate to get out on the lash and these shoes were amazing, just the job. Smart, good looking and would you believe it, a size 9 perfect fit and I felt a million dollars. Cinderella could go out on the piss after all! It was as if it was meant to be and I was ready to go out and do my best Riverdance impression because they felt so good.

But there was something nagging away in the back of my mind because it was going too well. Whose shoes were they - and why did they feel a little on the warm side? Something wasn't quite right so I thought I'd ask Mick where they had come from.

"Well Mr Marsh it's like this," he explained. "We saw your predicament with you needing a pair of shoes and as luck would have it, the man in room 302 died just 20 minutes ago. They're his shoes."

The lads were pissing themselves laughing and I just stood there open-mouthed not knowing what to do. How could I possibly go and get ratted knowing that some poor sod had popped his clogs and I was wearing them before he was even cold? I simply couldn't. Then I thought bollocks to it, he won't be needing them any more as the lure of the black stuff kicked in big time. Okay so there was perhaps a twang of guilt or conscience somewhere in the back of my mind, but I was determined we were going to have a good night and we bloody well did!

Next day reality hit me like a ton of bricks and I asked Mick if I could swap my trainers for the shoes but he declined. I asked if I could buy them, but again he said no. I suppose he was right, I mean imagine the poor bloke's family turning up to see the body and he's there without any shoes.

That's why whenever the lads saw me after that ready with my drinking head on they burst out laughing and from that day I have always been known at Wycombe as "Dead Man Walking". I dunno - the things you'll do for a beer.

CHEERS

Footballers are notorious for their antics off the field as much as on it and some of the stunts we have pulled you just would not believe. One great one that I was involved in concerned Walter Otta, an Argentinian player who joined Walsall when Ray Graydon was manager.

You have to realise that Ray, bless him, was a firm disciplinarian with the strictest codes of conduct I have ever known in football. For example he absolutely hated swearing and would fine us for bad language, he'd fine us if we turned up for work late or unshaven, did not wear regulation clothing, argued with referees, wore earrings or baseball caps, had mobile phones going off . . . in fact I reckon he would fine us for farting out of turn if he could.

He was always very sympathetic if you had problems and he went out of his way to try to help make foreign players settle down and feel welcome, part of the Bescot family if you like.

Now we sussed that Walter, who could hardly speak a word of English, was the perfect target for one of our pranks and as it was close to Christmas and he was living in digs a long way from his family, we thought it was odds-on that the gaffer would invite him for a proper traditional Christmas dinner at Graydon Towers. So we decided to teach Walter some English phrases that would come in handy when he was a guest in front of Mrs Graydon, granny Graydon and the rest of the family.

We were all in on the scam which started one day after training. We told Walter we would help him learn the lingo to become accepted and we managed to convince him that the perfect English phrase meaning "thank you" was "Cheers, you C**t". And when we said something was "f****** shit" that meant that it was "very nice indeed", while the polite English greeting when you meet somebody is to say "bollocks".

How we all kept straight faces I'll never know as Walter practiced and perfected his new English with the utmost vigour and enthusiasm. Every time he trotted out one of his new phrases we all grinned and gave him the thumbs-up every time he got it right, poor sod. He really thought he was starting to master the language and the trap was perfectly set.

And so as Christmas Day got closer we could barely contain ourselves at the thought of Walter saying "bollocks" when Ray opened the door, and "cheers you c**t" when he was handed his turkey and trimmings. And then following up with "that was f****** shit" afterwards. The boss would have blown a gasket big time. The closer the day got, the more hilarious we knew it was going to be and we just wished we could be a fly on the wall on the big day.

Sadly the best laid plan never came to fruition though. One afternoon we were given permission to have a drink in moderation because we hadn't got a game for a few days and a select gang of us, Walter included, found ourselves merrily chatting away at a bar in the town centre. It was one of those occasions when you are just glad to be out with your mates enjoying a pint with no pressure.

And then it happened. All of a sudden there was an almighty crash and all we saw was Walter reeling backwards at a great rate of knots clutching his mouth with blood pouring from it.

It turned out he had just bought a drink and, like Manuel in Fawlty Towers, decided to demonstrate his new-found mastery of the language to the barmaid. "Cheers you c**t", he said. And before you could say "bollocks" she had flattened him with a tremendous right hook that Tyson would have been proud of!

Our prank ended there and then - game over, scam in ruins. It was tremendous fun while it lasted though and it was a brilliant wheeze at the time, but then we had to stop laughing and look after Walter because the poor sod's mouth was in a bit of mess. We dusted him down, sorted him out and then, in true dressing room tradition, wished him all the best: Cheers, you ***t! He saw the funny side of it when we explained it to him and he took it all in good heart.

That was typical of the banter you get at football clubs and poor old Walter was not the only one to be on the receiving end of the Walsall piss-take. One year we were arranging our notorious players' Christmas party and told each one of our foreign contingent that it was fancy dress and advised them which pub we were meeting at. Okay so it was a mean trick to play but it was worth it just to see the amazed look on the ordinary punters' faces when King Arthur, a pantomime horse, Noddy and Batman all came crashing through the door into the bar and we howled with laughter. Priceless.

We've had some real jokers at the club but arguably John Hodge was the funniest. I've known lots of Scousers who think they are the dogs bollocks when it comes to humour, but I can assure you Hodgy was the real deal because he had us in stitches on so many occasions. His party trick was so gross - it involved certain bodily functions - that it made me want to throw up, but some of his other antics were hilarious.

We were playing at Bournemouth and had travelled down on a Friday. We stayed at a lovely hotel which had a little rock pool in the foyer near reception containing some koi carp.

We went out for a meal and Hodgy went straight back to the hotel afterwards, saying he needed the bog so I went for a walk and thought no more about it. I got back, went to bed like a good boy but had to answer a call of nature at about 2am. Standing there, half-asleep, I suddenly heard a whooshing sound that scared the crap out of me. In a dazed state I looked around wondering just what the hell it was then it came again. Whoosh.

I put the light on and it turned out that Hodgy had only taken all the koi carp out of the reception pool and put them in the bath for a joke. He was beside himself with laughter and said he had been waiting hours for me to go for a piss!

Another Scouser who made an impression, certainly on our manager at the time, Kenny Hibbitt, was Rod McDonald, a striker who thought he was the bee's knees. One day Kenny was standing by his car cursing which was unusual for him because he was always a laid-back character (until we lost, that is). As we were passing Rod asked what was the matter, and Kenny said he had locked his car with the keys still in the ignition.

Just look the other way a minute, said Rod. Within seconds there was a distinctive clunk noise and hey presto, the car was open. Evidently it was just one of the many "skills" he acquired in Liverpool as a lad, and many is the player who has had his mileage turned back a few thousand when it came to selling a car.

A player I got really close to at Walsall was a striker called Michele Cecere. As the name would suggest there was more than a trace of Italian about him and his dark eyes, jet black hair and Mediterranean type skin made him a real babe magnet. In fact Cec was engaged to an actress who had a starring role in Coronation Street (Jenny Bradley for those who can remember her) and they were very much in love so although he had plenty of offers, he always turned them down.

The trouble with Cec though was the fact that he couldn't hold his ale at all. Two pints and he was anybody's. We were out one night at the Waterfront in Merry Hill which has a big lake attached to it and before you knew it Cec was slurring his words and up for a late night dip in the lake. Now I don't know if you have ever tried arguing reasonably with someone who's drunk but it was well nigh impossible with him. He was insistent: He was going in the lake.

Okay you prat, I said. Down this pint in one and we will. I was banking on the fact he wouldn't be able to manage it and you could have knocked me down with a feather when he did. There was no going back now, I had to go through with it. It was like the end of the film Butch Cassidy and the Sundance Kid when they run out together, hand in hand. Only I was doing my Carl Lewis long jump impression and we made quite a splash.

The floodlights came on, there were security men all over the place and I half-expected the bloodhounds to be released. I don't know how but somehow we managed to clamber out without being caught and as luck would have it, a mate just happened to be passing in his car and we jumped in to complete the getaway. We sat in the back, took off our soaking clothes and headed for McDonald's - after all you do get peckish after a pint or six. We went for a drive through which was just as well considering our state of undress, but there was a twinkle in the eye of the girl who handed us our meal on the way out.

She was straining her neck to get a good look in the car and Cec asked what she was looking at. I dunno love, but I thought it might be interesting because your jeans are on the back window ledge of the car, she said.

While we all share a sense of humour, one thing the lads found hilarious but I certainly didn't was when I was bombarded with phone calls and letters from someone claiming to be my dad. It started off innocently enough when I came back from training one day and was told my father had rung the club.

Sensing something was wrong, I immediately rang my dad but when he said he hadn't phoned, I presumed it was just one of the lads playing a prank and thought nothing more of it. But then I started getting weird letters asking if I was alright, saying he hadn't seen me for a while and they were all signed 'your loving dad' and had a Bristol postmark.

This went on for six or seven months and I must admit I started to sympathise with people like Madonna who regularly attract stalkers. But me, a lower league football player? Nah. Something was definitely dodgy. It came to a head when we had to play Bristol City at Ashton Gate and by now the lads were winding me up something rotten. Hey Marshy, gonna see your Bristol dad? I was dreading it.

The coach swung into the car park and the police cordoned it off from the fans so we could make our way to the changing rooms. I deliberately took my time and was last off when all of a sudden someone broke through and ran up to me and asked: Is Chris Marsh on the coach because he's got some tickets for me. I'm his dad.

I didn't know this geezer from Adam so I said: "No, he's injured and didn't travel" and with that the bloke turned and walked away. That was the last I ever saw of him or heard from him. We made a few inquiries among the Bristol players and it turns out that the bloke who was stalking me had been involved in a car crash and had suffered some sort of brain injury, but why he should focus on me still remains a mystery to this day.

BOOZE

Booze has always played a part in my life one way or another and I am not the first player, and certainly won't be the last, to hold his hands up and say I could and should have done better without it. I can't help it, I just love beer and I enjoy the feeling it gives me. Only someone who drinks a lot can understand exactly where I'm coming from on that score but it is like a drug and so difficult to give up. I know because I've tried many a time to stay on the wagon with varying degrees of success.

I remember Neil Ruddock saying you could always tell who was the biggest boozer in the team because the others used to look up to him with respect. I was shy when I first set out in the pro ranks, but I could drink and that was my way of getting established and accepted. I could drink most of the other players under the table but nowadays that sort of culture has disappeared from the game almost totally.

The influx of foreign players has seen to that and that is no bad thing. People like Arsene Wenger the Arsenal manager have totally changed the face of British football and for the good I may add. Players are far better educated about booze, diet and fitness now and quite rightly so. The time-honoured footballers' daily routine of training, golf then pub have disappeared from the game.

Different people drink for different reasons. As I say, I happen to like it and it gave me some street cred in the dressing room. But it hasn't always been like that and I can pinpoint just where my career went into a downward spiral.

I had been in a run of consistently good form for Walsall, playing wide right, and had been getting some rave notices in the Press and as always when that happens, bigger clubs start to take an interest and check you out. There were all sorts of rumours flying around but one of them just would not go away - Liverpool were supposed to be very interested in me.

I thought here was my chance to make the big time and I was determined not to throw it away. I stayed sober, really applied myself and I remember when we played Rotherham away because it was probably my best performance in many a day. Everything I tried came off and I walked off the pitch thinking I know it's going to happen for me now, it's just a matter of when.

We all get one of those days when you can do no wrong and that was it for me. There was one incident that will remain in my memory for ever. The goalkeeper launched a kick downfield and in one move I brought it down dead, dipped my shoulder one way, swivelled and went the other leaving an opponent looking stupid, and slid an inch perfect pass through. It's the sort of thing you can do day after day in training yet in a match situation nine times out of 10 your touch lets you down and you end up looking a real plonker. Still the travelling Walsall fans went into raptures.

Next game we were at home and it was confirmed that there was a Liverpool delegation watching, including their chief scout Ron Yeats. And then . . . sod's law. I twisted awkwardly, did my cartilage and was out of action for two months. The transfer deadline passed and Liverpool manager Graeme Souness left Anfield in 1994. The rest is history.

I was so depressed my drinking went into overdrive and I hit the bottle in a big way. As a person I don't think I ever really recovered from seeing my hopes and dreams snatched away from me in such a cruel way. It's like winning the lottery and losing the ticket and even today it still hurts. A transfer then could have made me a millionaire.

There were times when I'd go off on a three-day bender and not know where I'd been. I desperately tried hard to kick it but it was always the crutch I used to lean on. It was always there for me and a source of comfort when times were rough. I had read about people such as Tony Adams, Paul Gascoigne, Jimmy Greaves, George Best and Paul Merson and I knew just what they had been through.

One night, the Walsall lads had been on a night out and ended up hurling a few beers down in a nightclub but one of our party kept on dropping his bottle. Surprisingly it was our goalkeeper Jimmy Walker who normally does have a safe pair of hands but on this occasion his hand-eye co-ordination seemed to desert him.

The bouncers - sorry doormen nowadays - asked him to leave in a not very subtle way and were not exactly genteel in the way they threw him out. In fact they were downright rough and I could see Wacka was going to get a good hiding because these blokes were pretty pissed off by now. It doesn't take much to get them annoyed.

I rushed out to try and calm things down - and that's the last I know because one of them smacked me on the back of the head with a bottle. I was out cold with blood gushing everywhere and then I had the strangest experience.

It was as if I was floating out of my body and I could look down and see all these people around me trying to revive me. It was utterly weird and for all intents and purposes I was dead. I felt calm, at ease and was genuinely ready to meet my maker. It was something like the film Ghost where dead people can look down on their bodies. I was doing that. I have never felt anything like it and I don't want to ever again.

21

However I must have come round eventually because I woke up in hospital with the most horrendous headache - like 20 hangovers rolled into one. I was detained in hospital for two days and needed 18 stitches in the gash on the back of my head. You can still see the scar now.

For once I had ended up in a scrap that was not my fault. Not that you could call it a scrap, really. It was a cowardly act by a thug of a bouncer who is lucky he did not have a death on his hands. You often read about footballers getting into scrapes at nightclubs and as long as there are gorillas like this bloke allowed to throw his weight around - and get away with it - then there will always be the sort of publicity none of us want.

One rule I never, ever broke though was no drinking on a Friday. It was one discipline I was always able to maintain because you do get found out and I could never let my team mates down like that. I was always able to look them in the eye after a game and say I had played my best, given everything and had never been hung over. That was important to me because we all rely on each other as players and if somebody was not pulling their weight for whatever reason, you could soon tell.

There was one day when I was at Northampton Town, four of us were in a car going to training. Me, John Hodge, John Frain and Darryl Burgess and there was a questionnaire in a newspaper asking for our honest answers to 20 questions about alcohol dependency. As we went through them the others ticked two or three boxes. I ticked 17 out of 20 and that's when I knew I had to get professional help.

I had been to Alcoholics Anonymous meetings and that didn't really help so I contacted Sporting Chance, an organisation backed by the PFA set up specifically for players such as myself . They told me that I should contact my local authority, they couldn't help. To me that was hugely disappointing to say the least. I thought they could have done more than that. Why should it matter whether I was Fred Bloggs from Rag Arse Rovers or one of the more high profile figures like Tony Adams? In my book we are all human beings with the same problem and deserve the same treatment.

I once attended, on Northampton's behalf, a presentation one night and had too much to drink, so much so that next morning on the way into work I was involved in a minor collision which ended with me reporting in for training stinking of booze and with blood all over my training top. Kevan Broadhurst, the manager at the time, wanted to sack me there and then and to be honest I couldn't have blamed him. However the Professional Footballers Association persuaded him to let me try counselling and surprisingly it seemed to work because I was dry for six months and started to feel good about myself.

It was all going so well too until the lads went to Cheltenham races. Big mistake. Well you can't go there and not have a Guinness can you and I got the taste for it again. Then it just seemed to develop into a vicious cycle: I'd have a drink, get rat-arsed somewhere and eventually go back home full of remorse for what a prat I'd been. I would behave myself, get back in the good books but then a couple of days later I'd be back in the pub and it would start all over again.

I just couldn't help myself because my body craved alcohol and it got so bad I started to feel really rough when I couldn't have a drink. Only someone who has been there can appreciate just how addictive it can be. It is an illness. Okay it's self-inflicted but an illness nonetheless and you, the victim, need specialist help. It's no good going to see a car mechanic and asking for a brain operation so you can't really expect a GP to tell you how to give up booze and get your life back on track.

Those around you who think it's dead easy to give it up just do not understand what you are going through. It is not something whereby you can click your fingers and you are cured. The alcoholic's motto, one day at a time, is the only mantra you can follow for that is why an alcoholic is never referred to as a former alcoholic; you can be 'dry' for years but all it takes is one drink and you are on the slippery slope again.

Whilst alcohol has got me into some scrapes, it has also provided some hilarious moments which I will take with me to the grave. Strangely enough, they all seem to stem from the players' Christmas parties.

There was one occasion when it was fancy dress - they nearly always are - and the majority of us decided to go as Elvis. We finished up at an Indian restaurant in Birmingham where an argument broke out and the police were called. You should have seen the looks on the coppers' faces when they stormed in to be confronted with 20 Elvis's, pissed out of their heads, having a go at each other and chucking poppadoms around like skimmers. Once they had finished laughing they managed to calm us down and get us out with no arrests thankfully. Typical Marshy though - I couldn't help remarking on the way out: Uh huh . . . Elvis is now leaving the building.

Another year, another fancy dress do and this time five of us went as the Village People with me being the American traffic cop. We had a great night, sang YMCA till we were blue in the face and everyone was ready for home. Not Marshy though. Oh no. I was a cop and was going to prove it.

Staggering all over one of the main roads into Wolverhampton, I managed to flag down at least half a dozen buses and tell the driver: Hey buddy I need to see your license and ID. Naturally they did not have them with them and so I ordered them to take them into the police station next morning. And you know what? Every single one of them agreed to.

I just wish I could have been there to see the desk sergeant's face when all those bus drivers turned up saying an American traffic cop had stopped them and ordered them to bring in their documents! To all the bus drivers in Wolverhampton: I bet you can't find the word gullible in the dictionary.

Then there was the time I had been to Glasgow for a testimonial match and because I wasn't actively involved, I was able to sample the world-renowned Scottish hospitality. Many pints and wee haufs later it was time to stagger off to bed but could I open the door to my room? It just wouldn't budge so in a drunken rage I started kicking the bloody door and hammering on it with my fists and I was taken aback when it eventually opened and there was a middle-aged man cowering behind it.

You could see the poor bloke was gripped in absolute terror but I suppose anyone would be at that time of day with the door taking such a battering. He clearly thought I was a psycho because he mumbled: Please, take anything you want only don't hurt me or my family. I looked in and saw a woman in her nightie with two young kids hiding behind her. I slurred out something of an apology and stumbled off, and eventually found the right room.

Without doubt though, my most embarrassing moment was returning home pissed one night in such a state, and having scoffed a doner kebab on the way, I threw up all over my future mother-in-law's head! Welcome to the family. That was one of many incidents that did not exactly go down well, and eventually my drinking has cost me my marriage. I remember that even before I got married my future brother-in-law would move his wardrobe against his bedroom door and barricade himself in to stop me going into his room and pissing over him because I had done that before in a drunken stupor.

For years I was a fool and got behind the wheel after drinking far too much. I got away with it - until recently that is. I took a wrong turn and found myself blocked by a barrier in the road and as I was turning the car round, Plod just happened to be right behind me. The consequence is that I was banned from driving and believe me, that is probably the best thing that could ever have happened to me because it made me realise just how stupid I have been. It's not until you're handcuffed and led into a police cell that the enormity of what you have done starts to hit home.

I am not proud and in fact I felt downright ashamed. I still do and now I have a criminal record as a reminder of my bad ways. I was a disgrace but believe me, I have learned my lesson. I went on a drink-drive rehab course afterwards and some of the information they throw at you about alcohol is frightening. It certainly had an impact on me and as long as I live, I will never drink and drive again.

The only saving grace from this whole sorry episode is that at least I have never hurt anyone which is probably more by luck than good judgment though. There are people who have killed when they've been driving while unfit and I could never live with myself if that had happened to me.

MARBELLA

Marbella - playground of the rich and beautiful people, the criminals . . . and occasional Walsall drunkards!

I bet there can't have been that many occasions in Walsall's history that the club have paid for the players to go on a short holiday abroad - and we certainly weren't going to miss the chance to enjoy ourselves.

We had beaten Peterborough to reach the fourth round of the FA Cup and the reward was a tie against Manchester United, a fixture that would guarantee the club a massive payday. It seemed odd that a club such as Walsall, which has always prided itself on such stringent housekeeping, could afford to push the boat out and pay for us to head for a break in Marbella. Still, we weren't going to look at any gift horses in the mouth and off we went.

The plan was to stay the night at Luton before catching an early flight out and the manager Jan Sorensen imposed a curfew so that we would be bright-eyed and bushy-tailed in the morning. I suppose he was still a bit naive if he thought us little band of angels would stay in and be tucked up with a good book by 8pm!

A group of us bunged the back door porter £50 to keep shtum and off we went in search of Luton's finest and most alcoholic. At the time I was still known as party pup because I hadn't developed into the fully-fledged party animal just yet, but I was working hard on that. We ended up in a nightclub and I foolishly paid the penalty for mixing my drinks and having them too quickly as well. Let's just say that relieving myself against the bar was not really such a good idea and the cold air really hit me when I was thrown out to leave me totally disorientated.

I stumbled into a taxi, half asleep and more than half drunk, and told the driver to take me home. "Where's that?" he asked. "Just head for junction 7 of the M6 and I'll take it from there," I slurred. The cabbie's eyes must have lit up at the thought of the fare he was going to pick up and didn't say a word. It wasn't until after an hour or so that I woke up and realised we were heading up the M6.

He wasn't too chuffed when I persuaded him to get off the motorway and head back for our hotel at Luton, but he cheered up when I eventually stumped up the £170 he asked for. The investment with the porter had proved handy too because he let me back in and I reckon I had two hours sleep, if that, before we were up for the flight.

On the way Sorensen had told us we were professionals with a big game coming up and he expected us to train hard for a few days with the promise of a night out at the end of it. Yeah right! We were out on the piss the first night there and found ourselves in a bar called Sinatras, throwing back the sangria and San Miguel as though it was going out of fashion.

The barman was a decent bloke, he looked after us and because we had got on so well we thought nothing of it when he asked for a photo of us all with him.

We behaved ourselves for the rest of the break, kept our noses clean, trained well and Sorensen, true to his word, said we had earned a night out and he was coming with us. He asked if we knew of anywhere to go and one or two suggested a place called Sinatras. We had never been there of course, but some of the locals had told us it was good and we ought to give it a go as it was one of the better watering holes.

In we went, Jan went up to the bar to get a round in and then we all clocked it at the same time and froze: The photo of us with the barman was behind the bar. Bollocks. We had been rumbled. We knew the gaffer had spotted it too and he was ready to explode because he sensed he had been stitched up. He was not a happy bunny and was just about to read the riot act when I had a brainwave - one of my better ones too.

Quick as a flash I called out: "Hey Pedro," and give him a big wink. "You still here you old bugger? Remember when a few of us met you four years ago? I see you've kept our photo though. Good man. Now do us a favour and let our gaffer get a round in then we can talk over old times."

Thankfully it worked. Pedro played along, the gaffer fell for it hook line and sinker and we all breathed a collective sigh of relief. If Jan had studied the picture closely, he would have realised that all the players on it could not have been there four years ago because he had only just signed some of them! And of the others, none of us looked four years older either.

Still we got away with it. We made sure Pedro had a good drink for keeping our secret and we proceeded to get pissed. Again.

It was while we were there that we came across the players from Rangers who were also on a mid-season break and I struck up a great friendship with Ally McCoist because our sense of humour was on the same wavelength. Among the Ibrox crew was the legendary Italian player Marco Negri and with my customary bravado I told the lads that I could talk Italian and I was going to speak to him in his native language.

Bets were being taken that I was bullshitting as usual and so I got Coisty to introduce me to Negri. There he was, resplendent in his duffel coat despite the heat, scruffy and unshaved, and I thought 'Christ, I'm not going to get away with this.' Still I had to go through with it. I couldn't lose face in front of this lot.

Striding towards him to greet him like a long-lost friend I hugged him, shook his hand vigorously and rattled off my best Italian. In fact it's my only Italian: "Dov'e l'ufficio postale".

Shit, that's it I thought as he looked at me as if he had trod in something. Then his eyes beamed as he suddenly realised what I was up to, embraced me back and gave me a warm greeting in Italian, much to the dismay of my mates who were gawping in disbelief. Was it any wonder he had looked surprised? After all, I had just asked: "Where is the post office"? Fortunately he had cottoned on and played along with it.

Marco and I continued to be best buddies for a while and to this day I haven't got a clue what he said back to me, but it did wonders for my street cred. Another Marbella scrape I got out of.

That was not the only time I was to meet up with the Rangers lads and in fact my friendship with Ally McCoist blossomed. He's one of the nicest blokes you could wish to meet. He really is a laugh, the life and soul of the party and in real life he's exactly how he comes across on the TV on A Question of Sport.

Nothing is too much trouble for him. In fact he would always look out for Walsall's results and would ring me to ask if I had scored. My missus secretly fancied him and when I told him, he would ring and say Marshy, put me on to Louise and he would give her the patter, as they say in Scotland. Then one day he told her to dress me in a Rangers shirt, make love to me and pretend it was him. Huh. Great idea that was for 20 seconds!

I found myself in a bar chatting with Coisty and Ron Atkinson, who just mentioned in passing that he was on the lookout for a new striker. You could see the light bulb come on above Ally's head. His eyes lit up, he could sniff a chance and he did his best to persuade Ron that he could do a job for him.

The conversation went:
AM: I could be the answer to your problems, big man.
RA: Yeah, you've got a good record but only up here in Scotland. That's pub football really. Reckon you could hack it in England?
AM: Aye, of course I could. I've been top scorer in Scotland several times and just look at my international record.
RA: But you've got a few miles on the clock now, old son.
AM: True, but I'm still fit.
RA: Not sure if you've got the pace any more.
AM: Pace? I've still got plenty of pace. I'm one of the sharpest at the club.
RA: You reckon?
AM: Aye, I'm sure.
RA: So you're still nippy then?
AM: No doubt at all. I've still got it over the first few yards. I'm your man.

That was it. He had been suckered. He thought he was in when Ron scratched his head, drew breath in through clenched teeth, looked him up and down and then came out with a real howler:

"Well in that case, run up to the bar and get me a lager!"

Coisty was done up like a kipper but took it in great spirit as you would expect and laughed as much as anyone in the room. And that's typical of the man. He is so humble and down to earth and treats everybody the same - with respect. In fact in all the years I have known him, I've never once heard him say anything derogatory about arch rivals Celtic and that tells you everything about the guy.

THE MEDIA

One career I had thought of taking up when I left the pro game was getting into the media, but sadly that never happened which is a shame because I really enjoyed my little spell doing a column each week during my playing days.

The job in question was giving a regular rundown on life behind the scenes at Walsall and it appeared every Saturday in the Sporting Star which I believe is one of the few Saturday sports papers still in existence.

Each week I would either phone or meet up with whoever was covering Walsall at the time and spill the beans on my team mates, revealing the dark secrets they didn't want the world to know about! While it was great fun, it also made me aware of just where to draw the line and how far I could go with the piss-take.

At Bescot we had some really easy targets it was like shooting fish in a barrel, and it was great to see the players' faces on Monday after you had slaughtered them in print on the Saturday.

One thing I never did though, was rip the piss out of somebody who had had a bad game the week before, and I never said anything that would hurt or upset a player either. It was all done in fun, nothing serious, but I must have done it right because after I had done my stint, I had loads of letters from both Walsall fans and ordinary supporters saying how much they had enjoyed reading my words of wisdom.

I'm sure that having the respect of the dressing room helped. I know I've had the odd session or two but I couldn't turn up pissed or they would slaughter me - I had to behave or they would find some way of ridiculing me in public. They'd only have to pass the ball to me to do that!

Now I know I'm never going to be the next Harry Harris, but that stint in the Sporting Star helped me see things from a different prospective - from the outside looking in as it were. I know from the feedback I got from the reporters at the time that they thought I had done a decent job, and it was a thoroughly enjoyable experience.

I also saw things from a newspaper's point of view and it all helped me understand just what it means to be taken into a journalist's confidence. You get to know the reporter just as well as your team mates and know who you can trust and who you can't. Luckily I have never been stitched up but I know plenty of players who have. Let's face it, a reporter can ruin your career in a paragraph.

Some reporters I would trust with my life; others I wouldn't piss on them if they were on fire. But I believe that what goes around comes around and I know that if I had ever got the move to Liverpool, I know which journalists I would have spoken to exclusively and which ones I would have ignored because trust cuts both ways.

Now not many people know this, but I have actually worked for the News of the World and no - it wasn't one of those sleazy kiss and tell stories about footballers that always seem to end up there.

We had been playing at Fulham and as usual I was first out of the showers and into the bar. I was just getting the glass of orange juice (yeah right) to my lips when a badly out of breath man in what looked like a flasher's mac plonked himself next to me.

I thought he was ready to have a heart attack but he just managed to blurt out that he had been badly held up in traffic, but had to do a brief report for the News of the World. He had managed to cobble together the nitty-gritty of the game, such as the result and who had scored, but there was another important piece which he needed to do and that was give marks out of 10 for each player's performance. He didn't know who I was and obviously thought I was one of the Press corps because I had made it quickly to the bar (see, it's not just us footballers who have a reputation!). He asked if I could help him out and rate the players performances.

Well that was an opportunity far too good to miss. You know what? Every one of the Walsall players had had an absolute mare and they all got three or four out of 10, maximum. That was except the outstanding player, easily man of the match, best player on the pitch by a distance, he's too good for this lot and ought to be playing for Real Madrid . . . yep, none other than Chris Marsh who was given a mark of nine! You can just imagine the stick I got off the lads when they read the paper the next day.

I don't suppose I'll be getting a Christmas card off Johnny Wilkinson who I was lucky enough to meet on another trip to London at a media bash. I happened to be introduced to him at a function one night and I didn't know him from Adam. Anyway he asked me who I was so I told him and who I played for. He then told me he was a rugby player but I just shrugged my shoulders and said: Never heard of you sorry.

That is unusually arrogant of me and anyone who knows me will vouch for the fact that I'm not normally like that. Let's face it, I've done nothing to be proud of really.

So you can just imagine the amount of stick I got when Wilkinson dropped the goal that won England the rugby world cup in Australia. My mates couldn't help themselves. Who the f**k is he now Marshy? Ever heard of him? Remember the name now? Yeah okay, okay. I know. I wonder if he remembers me. Perhaps not.

But I would like to put it on record that despite my less-than-courteous greeting he did not treat me with anything less than good grace which is what you come to expect from most of the rugby lads. They all seem to be a different breed - there is none of the big-headed snobbishness about them that you seem to get in other sports, particularly football when players make it to the top.

Wilko remains one of my heroes and I'm proud to have met him. I just wish he could get over the injuries that have plagued him non-stop since that wonderful day when England got their name on the other world cup. I can watch his kick in the dying seconds over and over again and it still sends shivers down my spine.

I've quite got into rugby since I finished playing and I am continually flabbergasted at the different culture between the sports. Before the match against New Zealand in November I was in a pub near the ground when a huge bloke accidentally bumped into me, spilling what little was left in my glass.

Quick as a flash there was a fresh pint in front of me and he was still apologising 10 minutes later. The upshot was we ended up buying each other drinks for quite some time before we left for the game having become the best of mates. You can imagine what would have happened had we been football fans out on the piss before a match. I think it may have been different slightly.

While I accept I am no expert on the game of egg-chasing, people like Martin Johnson are, and when a world cup winning captain comes out and criticises the coach you have to take on board what he is saying. England have had a really bad run of results and it's a fact that if it happened in football, the man in charge would have been sacked some time ago. I think Andy Robinson was more than a touch fortunate to have remained in charge as long as he did and I hope that whoever takes over has enough time to knock the team into shape before the next world cup.

As I said Wilkinson is one of my heroes and I was particularly saddened to see Charlie Hodgson being dubbed as the new Wilko. In my mind he's not fit to lace his boots and never will be. Wilko showed nerves of steel with his match-winning kick, yet Hodgson misses kicks from simple positions quite regularly.

It's all about bottle. In football anyone can take a penalty when your team is 5-0 up because it doesn't matter, but when it's 0-0 in the dying seconds, that's a different type of pressure altogether and that's why Wilkinson would get my vote every time. He is sheer class.

Ray of Sunshine?

Ray Graydon, as I've mentioned elsewhere, was a real stickler for the rules and there were times when I thought of setting up a direct debit to pay my fines because I was in trouble that much. I'm convinced he had me marked down as the ringleader, the chief troublemaker, and it seemed I was always the first he picked on when anything went wrong.

Sometimes I deserved it, sometimes I was innocent, but he was always consistent: I was top of his hit list! To be honest he and I just didn't see eye to eye off the pitch. I thought his man management was absolutely hopeless but I will be the first to put my hand up and say that as a coach he was absolutely exceptional and got the very best out of every single player under his command.

In a strange way I like Ray because he certainly improved me as a player, there's no doubt about that. One thing's for sure - he'll go down in history as one of the most successful managers Walsall have ever had and you cannot take that away from him. The fans loved him too, nicknamed him Sir Ray, and they virtually gave him the freedom of Walsall when he took the club into the First Division (now the Championship) after beating Reading in the play-off final at Cardiff.

It's interesting to note that when he took over the Saddlers, his first achievement was to keep them in the division and I well remember fans

39

dressed up as characters from the Great Escape. We cornered the market before Albion did when they managed to stay up! After that there was the glory at Cardiff and it's amazing how things have turned around, with Walsall sliding into football's bottom division while the side they beat that day having gone on to establish themselves in the Premiership under Steve Coppell.

As I say Ray cost me a lot of money during his spell at Bescot. He gave Darren Wrack and me permission to go the PFA Awards in London one year when we were both injured and you could see it in his eyes that he knew we would end up in trouble. He told us we had to be back in for training at 11am the next day or we would be fined a week's wages.

So off we went, had a brilliant night, drank plenty of course and as we made our way to bed at 5am we asked the hotel desk clerk for an alarm call at 7.30 so we would be back in time. There didn't seem much point going to sleep for a couple of hours but we were both knackered and fell off straight away.

Wracky woke first, looked at his watch and shouted: Marshy, it's 9 o'clock! I've never sobered up so quickly. We raced down to reception and started to give the woman on the desk a bollocking for not waking us, but she apologised profusely and explained that the computer system had crashed in the early hours and they couldn't get it back up.

We ordered a taxi and a bloody great Mercedes with tinted windows turned up. Passers-by were probably expecting to see Madonna or some other superstar leaving the Grosvenor Hotel at 9.30, not a couple of hung-over football players, but we set off having been told it would cost us £200. The driver was great and when we explained our position, we said there would be a few extra quid in his pocket if he could get us back to Walsall by 11am.

Well he had a great try, bless him, and he drove like Schumacher with his foot to the floor all the way up the motorway. We arrived at the training ground just 10 minutes late as the players were ambling out in dribs and drabs and we were immediately summoned into the gaffer's office.

We knew exactly what was coming. Wracky, to be fair, had used his mobile to phone Ray on the way back to tell him of our predicament, but he didn't want to know and hung up so we knew he was going to be gunning for us.

We tried to convince him of the truth, that the hotel computer had broken down, but he was having none of it and simply refused to believe it, even though we begged him to ring the hotel to confirm our story. So that was it - a week's wages docked, a £220 bill for the taxi - I gave the driver £20 anyway for his valiant effort - and just to rub salt into the wounds the rest of the players were excused training that day and were going paintballing instead! We were gutted.

When Wracky joined the club, we became firm friends virtually from the minute he walked through the door and my heart went out to him when he suffered a broken leg at Yeovil last season. When I heard of his injury I made the customary phone call that all footballers do. I rang him and said: Good and bad news Wracky. Bad news is it looks like a terrible injury. The good news is I've sold your boots.

It didn't seem so funny though when the extent of his injury was discovered and at one stage we all feared his career might be over because it was such a bad break. No-one is more delighted than me to see him back in the team and fit again. He is due a testimonial at the end of the season and it's hard to believe he's been at Walsall for 10 years, but there again he is part of the furniture nowadays.

A favourite story of mine about Wracky was a night match at Portsmouth. I don't know why but he had had this certain feelgood factor all day and when we got to the ground he said he fancied backing himself to score the first goal. Now as everyone knows there are laws against players betting on football matches they take part in so a few mates got a little syndicate together and whacked some money on Darren at 10-1 to be the first goalscorer.

Poor lad. He was trying shots from the halfway line, was taking all the corners and free kicks, desperate to get a goal. And then it happened. He hammered a free kick right into the top corner - an absolute gem of a goal and you can imagine his delight as he celebrated like there was no tomorrow. The fans must have been wondering why we were all so excited, jumping around as if we had won the league. Only one thing ruined it for us though. We were hammered 5-1!

On another occasion we were having a break in Ayia Napa and for some reason we had been booked into a four star hotel instead of the usual rough and ready accommodation reserved for footballers who would be going out on the lash. It was so posh the lads could not believe it and they started taking bets on who would misbehave and get us all kicked out. No need to guess who was odds-on favourite - and I duly obliged!

It had started badly and went downhill. It was another of those occasions when I was going abroad with the lads and simply had to set the standard. I managed to get half-pissed before we even got on the plane and I spent the entire flight throwing up into the sick bag. The family sitting next to me just thought I was a poor traveller and said I would be all right when the plane landed. Bless 'em, they probably didn't expect a professional footballer to be rat-arsed at that time of the morning and who could blame them?

On the first night we managed to drink the bar dry and I somehow managed to end up fast asleep in a corridor. The lads took pity, gathered me up and put me to bed thinking I had just had too much and they would let me sleep it off. But it was only a matter of a few hours before they were calling me all the names under the sun and kicking me out of bed because evidently there had been a stack of complaints and the hotel had woken up Ray to tell him that certain people in his group had not

The hairstyle dates this to Chris's early days at Walsall in 1987

Chris in 1989 without the long hair

Top: Gracing the same pitch as Beckham
Bottom: Andy Cole shows his class as Marshy is left in his wake

45

Top: During his spell at Northampton Town
Bottom: Chris during his brief Wycombe spell agains Wigan

46

Top: Chris gets stuck in!
Bottom: Promotion celebrations in 1999.

47

Celebrating the winning goal for promotion against Oldahm Athletic 1999

2000-2001 Season against Wolves at Molineux.

Chris during the Chris Nicholl days

Top: With Ally McCoist, Adrian Viveash and Jimmy Walker
Bottom: With Paul Gascoigne, Adrian Viveash and Jimmy Walker

51

Top: With Steve Bull on opening "Bostin Baps" after finishing playing
Bottom: With Chris Nicholl and Frank Worthington

1994 - Injury means the Liverpool opportunity is missed

Chris in a local derby against West Brom

Binning the boots before starting his own business

Testimonial year 1996

Liverpool to move in for Chris Marsh

Liverpool are poised to make a shock £300,000 swoop for Walsall's play-anywhere Chris Marsh.

The fallen Premier League giants have watched the Sedgley-born player twice in the last three weeks and are expected to follow up with a firm bid.

I spoke to their representative after the game against Doncaster last week and he confirmed the club's interest.

Originally they were attracted to Bescot by young midfielder Dave Edwards, along with Arsenal, Manchester United, Spurs and Coventry.

But they were impressed by the versatile Marsh, and Saddlers will be only too happy to sell to ease cash-flow problems.

Marsh, 22, has played in virtually every position for Walsall apart from central defence and goalkeeper, and has emerged as a skilful ball-player central to manager Kenny Hibbitt's plans.

He has improved this season and has been one of Saddlers' most consistent performers in their battle to stay with the Third Division promotion hopefuls.

It is known Hibbitt rates Marsh highly, but a fee in the region of £300,000 would enable him to buy new players to bolster the promotion challenge.

EXPRESS & STAR, FRIDAY, NOVEMBER 6, 1992

EXPRESS & STAR, MONDAY, NOVEMBER 9, 1992

Liverpool eyes stay on Marsh

By Chris Smith

Walsall look to be headed for a major cash influx with £300,000-rated midfielder Chris Marsh being tracked by Liverpool.

Liverpool despatched two scouts to Bescot on Saturday to make further checks on Marsh, who did well against Scarborough even though he was playing out of position at fullback.

Manchester United, Everton, Norwich, Oldham, Coventry and Villa were also represented, along with Derby and Albion.

But the Anfield side are expected to follow up with a firm bid — and Saddlers will not stand in his way.

Chairman Jeff Bonser repeated at today's annual meeting that manager Kenny Hibbitt must generate his own income for team strengthening.

He said that while the club had cut their losses from £449,000 to £29,000, it did not mean Hibbitt could plunge into the transfer market for new players.

"The club must generate outside income and be able to stand on their own two feet," he said. "We have seen what has happened at Birmingham and we must now allow that to happen here.

Bonser said the club were close to clinching a deal to lease out an advertising sign facing the M6 which would bring in around £100,000 a year, they were pursuing the installation of an all weather pitch and changing rooms for community use, while director Mike Lloyd was working on engaging acts for a summer music festival at the stadium.

EXPRESS & STAR, FRIDAY, NOVEMBER 6, 1992

Liverpool to swoop for £300,000 Marsh

By Chris Smith

Liverpool are poised to make a shock £300,000 swoop for Walsall's play-anywhere Chris Marsh.

The fallen Premier League giants have watched the Sedgley-born player twice in the last three weeks and are expected to follow up with a firm bid.

I spoke to their representative after the game against Doncaster last week and he confirmed the club's interest.

Originally they were attracted to Bescot by young midfielder Dave Edwards, along with Arsenal, Manchester United, Spurs and Coventry.

But they were impressed by the versatile Marsh, and Saddlers will be only too happy to sell to ease cash-flow problems.

Marsh, 22, has played in virtually every position for Walsall apart from central defence and goalkeeper, and has emerged as a skilful ball-player central to manager Kenny Hibbitt's plans.

He has improved this season and has been one of Saddlers' most consistent performers in their battle to stay with the Third Division promotion hopefuls.

It is known Hibbitt rates Marsh highly, but a fee in the region of £300,000 would enable him to buy new players to bolster the promotion challenge.

Veteran defender Colin Methven will return to the Walsall defence tomorrow — with orders to make it noisy.

Methven, missing all season with a calf injury, will play if he feels fit, and manager Kenny Hibbitt is leaving the decision up to the player.

But he will have to start without first-choice fullbacks Wayne Williams (thigh) and Derek Statham (hamstring) so youngster Richard Knight will be drafted in and Steve O'Hara switched to cover for Statham.

Wayne Clarke is expected to lead the attack having missed the 3-0 defeat at Barnet because of flu.

The rumours of Chris's big money move.

57

Marsh tops target list

Walsall's exciting, goal-laden season has brought the scouts flocking to Bescot and the signs are manager Kenny Hibbitt could face a battle to hang on to his best players.

While Saddlers' priority on the pitch must be promotion, everyone knows financial stability of the club is even more important and a sale or two would put them in a very healthy position.

Apart from Neil Tolson's move to Oldham, Walsall have not made any money on transfer dealings but the indications are that trend might soon be reversed.

And there are quite a few of the current crop of players who could fetch a bob or two on the transfer market, leaving Hibbitt with money to spend on new faces as well as the satisfaction of knowing he has done his bit to keep the club afloat.

Exactly how much cash would be given to him remains to be seen, but he could be forgiven for licking his lips at the sort of fees he could demand for his staff.

Players such as Mark Gayle who has established himself as one of the lower divisions' best goalkeepers. He cost £15,000 and it would not be unreasonable to expect another nought on that figure if he were to move.

Dean Smith and Steve O'Hara have both showed they have the potential to play at a higher level while a handful of

Premier League clubs continue to monitor the progress of Dave Edwards.

Mike Cecere is playing the best football of his career at the minute, Rod McDonald's scoring power will always stimulate interest and of course there is the jewel in the crown — Wayne Clarke.

But the man of the moment is Chris Marsh, with Liverpool heading the queue.

Marshy has struggled to win the critical fans over but they will surely appreciate he has been one of Walsall's most consistent players this season — in any position.

It is not easy to tag a player as versatile without hinting that he might be a jack of all trades and master of none.

Confidence

But in Marsh's case it is a fitting description because he has slotted in a number of positions and done equally well.

His skill on the ball is exceptional and it is a refreshing change to see a player have the confidence to attempt to dribble his way out of trouble.

"I've had quite a few rollickings from the boss for not just thumping the ball away, but that's the way I like to play," he says.

"I like to get involved and there's nothing I enjoy better than running at people with the ball. But the gaffer's always telling me there's a time and place for everything and he doesn't like

to see players fiddling around with the ball too close to their penalty area."

Marsh is quick to point out that his improved form is in no small measure down to the influence of Derek Statham at left back.

"He's always telling me what to do and where to be. There's no doubt he has lifted my game.

"Kevin MacDonald has also taken me to one side and with players like those two, plus Wayne Clarke, you can't help but learn from their experience and it's been of great benefit to me personally."

He is adamant that any transfer speculation will not get to him though. "I'm extremely flattered to be told clubs are watching me and they don't come any bigger than Liverpool.

"It's nice to be talked about and it gives me a real buzz to know scouts are watching, but I can honestly say I will not let it affect me.

"I owe Walsall everything and all I want to do is continue to play as well as I possibly can for them. I love the club and there are some very good players here.

"It's a tremendous atmosphere in the dressing room and I think they are the best players I have ever been involved with. It would be a big wrench to leave them because they are all mates.

"But I'm not counting any chickens and if I'm still here at the end of the season I will be quite happy because I'm sure we will be celebrating promotion."

Barnes may be on his way out

★ **JOHN BARNES** may be on his way out of Liverpool soon – for £1.5million.

Graeme Souness, tackling a major rebuilding job, is reluctant to sell but may test the market ahead of Barnes' reaching the end of his contract next year.

Barnes, who had a workout in the A-team yesterday, has a contract that limits his fee to around that £1.5 million figure.

Souness has also made a firm inquiry for **Chris Marsh,** Walsall's £300,000-rated midfielder.

exactly endeared themselves to the rest of the hotel guests.

Well to this day I certainly can't remember stripping naked, booting the door of every single room in the hotel, puking all over the place and falling asleep in a corridor, but evidently I must have done because people had moaned about having to step over a starkers, snoring wreck! Needless to say I was fined again and we were asked to leave the hotel immediately.

By now Ray had begun to get it into his head that I was a bit of a scamp and when he heard that some Walsall players had got involved in trouble when they had gone to see Mike Tyson fighting in Manchester, he instinctively knew who would be involved. Only this time I left him angry and frustrated.

Yes, there had been a spot of bother at the hotel the 10 of us were staying at which had ended up with the manager and myself stumbling to the ground holding on to each other. It certainly hadn't been a fight and Tyson was never in any danger, but it was just one of those things that had looked funny to the people with us at the time and would have been a great picture for the paparazzi. But the fact is when they had stopped laughing seven of the lads went out for a meal and I went back to my room to freshen up and change after rolling around on the floor. After enjoying their meal, another incident occurred on returning to the hotel.

Word got back to Ray that there had been an incident and he insisted on having the CCTV sent down so he could see for himself what had happened. You should have seen his face when it showed the ringleader - me - going back into my hotel room at a respectable time and sober as a judge. He was gutted he couldn't pin that one on me and fine me again.

Probably the most notorious incident though was the time I drove the club minibus away and hid it at Lilleshall where we were training. We were in the middle of a really bad run of results at the time and players were feeling quite depressed, and I was trying desperately to think of ways to lift their spirits and put some bounce back into their step.

I noticed that Tom Bradley, the club physio at the time, had left the bus parked with the keys in the ignition so that was it. I got in and drove round the training ground, blowing the horn at the players and they were in fits of laughter. Little things please little minds but at least it helped to lighten the gloom lurking around the place.

I parked the minibus behind some hedges so it was really hidden and Tom was absolutely mortified when he turned up and realised it wasn't where he had left it. Now Tom is a great bloke who was very popular with the players, but he is one of life's natural worriers and so easy to wind up. He flew into a blind panic and immediately went running to the gaffer who said nobody would be going until the culprit had owned up.

As soon as I stuck my hand up Ray said: I knew it would be you. You're fined. I tried to explain I had done it as a joke but he did not see the funny side of things and that was another week's wages down the drain.

The best of it was though, we were playing Birmingham City on the Friday night and the match was being shown live on Sky TV. As the teams were being put up on the screen the Sky commentator tried to impress the nation with his insight into the club and said: And at number seven for Saddlers is Chris Marsh, who nicked the bus and drove it away from the training ground in midweek.

So that was it, the whole country knew now. Ray had leaked to one of the local reporters what had happened and the Sky crew had picked it up from there. But in a way I stole his thunder because I had already written my column in the Sporting Star in which I owned up to the incident and said why I had done it. It was a way of getting my retaliation in first.

When my daughter Harriet was born, I followed the age-old tradition of wetting the baby's head and took some of the lads out on a bender. Tom was good enough to drive us around on a pub crawl and after hitting several watering holes in Wolverhampton, we carried on to Birmingham where my mates did their best to get me blind drunk.

They filled a half-pint glass with a shot from each of the optics and that must have had some sort of effect because all of a sudden I turned into a social hand grenade and someone had pulled the pin. We were heading back home in the minibus and I noticed one of my shoes was missing.

All of a sudden I was not Mr happy-go-lucky and became Mr Angry. I said that unless my shoe was returned by the count of 10 a bottle was going through the window. The lads laughed and actually delivered the countdown, believing I wouldn't go through with it. That was it: Three, two, one - and then I hurled a bottle of Budweiser with such force it went straight through the side window of the minibus. People walking along Broad Street - one of Birmingham's most busy city centre hotspots - must have wondered what the hell was happening with a flying bottle and glass everywhere coming from a passing vehicle.

The next day Tom, still worried about the state of the minibus, told the gaffer that a stone had somehow gone through the window and it had been an accident. I did not really expect him to cover up my boozy escapade but he did and I thanked him for saving me yet another few quid!

I managed to save my team-mate Ian Roper a few quid as well because on every Monday morning it was a compulsory weigh-in, when every player had their weight checked to make sure they hadn't been overindulging and were keeping themselves in tip-top trim. Ray's punishment was a fine of £10 for every pound the player was overweight.

The trouble was, Ray also insisted in using a body mass index test as well where you were fined if you were a certain percentage over the recommended BMI. Ropes, poor sod, has a perfect physique for the BMI and there is not an ounce of fat on him, but Ray had set him an impossible weight target and he was 8lbs over every Monday. We were not exactly on massive wages at Walsall and £80 a week was a lot to be losing, so I, as the PFA representative, managed to negotiate a reduction in the weight target and it ended with Ropes shelling out just £40 a week instead.

We all dreaded those Monday mornings and I used to make a point of not eating or drinking anything after 5pm on the Sunday, and then having a long sauna session at a hotel near the ground. It was amazing how many others did that too while some went for a run in a wet suit to sweat off the excess pounds and on one occasion a player who shall remain nameless - okay then it was Dean Keates - actually hid the scales. Needless to say Ray had a Plan B in place though and always kept a spare set just in case.

There have been countless other times when Ray and I crossed swords, such as when I decided after a couple of sherberts that I would be a rock star and trash the hotel room I was staying in. I had just lifted the television above my head and was about to hurl it out of the window when the door sprang open and in walked Ray with immaculate timing. Now I can't imagine why, but he just didn't believe me when I said all I was trying to do was get a better reception for the picture.

He may have been a right so and so to work with, but I will always be grateful to Ray because I played my best football under him and I know most of the players at the club felt the same way. His style of management, along with that of Chris Nicholl and Lawrie Sanchez, was to keep the players at arm's length and not get close to any of them.

Getting that happy medium is so hard for a manager. Do you get close to the players? If you do, do you lose that bit of respect and control over them? If you are too hard on them they might rebel. Some players need an arm around them, whilst others need a kick up the backside to provoke a reaction and get the best out of them. It's a hard job and you need a bit of everything. That's why in my opinion, the best managers I played under were Ray Graydon, Chris Nicholl and Lawrie Sanchez. At a higher level, you only have to look at Mourinho, Fergusson and Wenger, whose teams are packed with superstars who work their socks off for their managers because they have the X-Factor.

THE BUTLER NEARLY DID IT

I've always got on well with the Walsall fans and had a good rapport with them, especially those I met in the bar after games! Even during matches they would take the piss when I did one of my trademark step-overs. I think they loved it as much as I did and it was all good fun and banter.

By and large they are great fans who stick by the club through thick and thin. If they like you, you are one of their heroes and always will be but if you are not, well they can make life difficult for you. Take Martin Butler for instance. He is one of my best mates in football and I'm delighted to see him back at Bescot and doing well. I really hope he gets over 20 goals this season and help takes them to promotion because you could not meet a nicer lad.

We are from the same neck of the woods, joined Walsall as youngsters and we both made our debuts having come through the ranks, but for some reason the crowd had never really taken to Butts during his first spell with the club, although generally they do love their own home grown players. He admitted he felt a little apprehensive when Richard Money wanted to sign him for the club again and he asked my advice.

I told him that I too had had my fair share of stick from the terraces when I started out and it's something you just have to put up with because it comes with the territory for a football player. It is up to you, the player, to turn things around and convince the fans that you're not a mug and you really want to do well for the club.

I think it's fair to say it has nothing to do with your ability. Sometimes it's just a matter of whether your face fits or not. I remember telling Butts about the time I was having unbelievable stick from the crowd. I was having a stinker of a game, and quite rightly, my number came up as a substitution - anyone outside the ground would have thought Walsall had scored because the cheer that went up was deafening! I think telling that story helped Butts, because it showed how you can turn a crowd around by keeping on trying, you can earn their respect.

Butts is a great player, but also a great person. I love him to death, and he has been a hero at all his previous clubs. Coming back to Walsall to prove some people wrong has taken guts. I remember just before his departure, he was played at left back up at Blackpool and took some horrible stick despite being played badly out of position by the manager who should probably have taken the blame!

Butts moved on, which was probably the right thing to do at the time and played for various clubs and yet it was me who prevented him from joining Wolves, the team he supported since he was a kid. It was in 1997 that the pair of us looked likely to leave Walsall who were asking £25,000 for him and a bit more than that for me and we ended up at Cambridge who were managed by Roy McFarland.

Roy was really keen to sign Butts and had virtually agreed a deal after he had played for their reserves, but I was not allowed to play by Walsall in case I got injured and any deal may have been jeopardised. It was just at that time that Martin started getting messages from his mum saying Mark McGhee had rung from Wolves and was interested in talking to him.

When somebody with a Scottish accent started ringing the hotel asking to speak to Butts, he thought it was me and the rest of the lads having a joke and refused to take the calls. One night, being the good pro that he is, he stayed in the hotel while I went out on the lash and returned having had the odd orange juice or three!

I was crashed out snoring my head off when the phone rang again. Butts somehow managed to wake me and told me to get rid of the caller because he was getting pissed off with it by now and didn't think it was funny any more. I took the phone off him and said: "Look mate, this isn't funny any more now just f**k off and leave him alone." That's done the trick, I thought. Next morning the hotel had another message that Mark McGhee had rung and left a private phone number for Butts to call back. He really thought this was getting quite tiresome by now and of course, he didn't bother to return the call.

Later that day Roy and Butts sat down to try and thrash out a deal and they told me to sod off out for a beer which was, of course, a real hardship. While I was throwing a few down I thought, just out of curiosity, I would ring the number to try and find out just who it was being a pain in the arse because this had gone on for quite a few days now.

You can imagine the rest. Yep, the voice on the other end was indeed Mark McGhee and yes, he did want to talk to Butts. I raced back to the hotel where Butts had already signed the deal and he was a Cambridge player. It happened that quickly.

You should have seen Martin's face when I told him he had just missed the chance of joining his beloved Wolves. Sorry, mate!

That's not the only time I have screwed up and made things bad for Butts after I've been drinking. There was one occasion when I called round at his flat and somebody rang the doorbell. I opened it and there were three lads standing there looking quite menacing as if they had come for trouble.

Well after a pint or two you think you are Lennox Lewis and I told these three to sod off because I would fight them with one hand tied behind my back. My Incredible Hulk impression must really have scared the crap out of them because they started to walk away but could I leave it there? Oh no. I had to carry on.

It was at the time Eric Cantona had jumped into the crowd at Selhurst Park with a kung fu kick and I thought 'anything he can do, I can do better' so I sprinted after them, used a little wall as a launch pad and went flying through the air, aiming to take them all out with one of my best Jackie Chan kung-fu moves. The only thing was the booze impaired my direction somewhat and instead of flattening these innocent blokes who meant no harm, I ended up in a mid air collision with a parked car and came off second best.

To make things worse, these three then realised what my intentions had been and seeing me there in a heap on the floor, decided to kick the shit out of me! I suppose I deserved it and it was only when I was being patched up that I found out they had called round to see their mate - Martin's brother-in-law. Oops.

Despite all that, Butts and I are still friends . . . . I think!

Football's a fickle old game

Football's a fickle old game. One minute you're the best thing since sliced bread, the next you're a complete tosser and it's all about opinion. And when you're a manager, you hold a player's livelihood in the palm of your hand.

I've played under 14 different managers and it's amazing how different they are in the way they go about their jobs. If a new gaffer doesn't rate you he will soon move you on out of the club and the chances are your career could be in ruins just on one man's whim.

You can be the best player in the world, but if he doesn't think you're any good and can't do the job he wants you to, then you're on the way towards the scrap heap. It can be for just saying one word out of place, or saying the wrong thing at the wrong time, but some I know are utterly ruthless who do not give a second thought about a player or his career.

Fortunately I can look back on my career with a lot of pride. I have enjoyed every minute of being a professional player which brought three promotions and three relegations at Walsall and I was lucky enough to have been awarded a benefit for 10 years' service with the club.

Staying that length of time in one place is quite rare nowadays although having said that Ian Roper, Jimmy Walker and Darren Wrack, all team-

69

mates during my spell at Walsall, have all chalked up 10 years with the Saddlers which shows how loyal they have been, and in return how good the club have been in looking after their staff.

The owner Jeff Bonser and chief executive Roy Whalley were good to me and helped keep costs down during my testimonial season. I know they have their critics, but they have always had the best interests of the club at heart. It is a well-known fact that if it had not been for Jeff, Walsall would have been sunk years ago. Ask yourself: Would you risk your finances bailing out a football club? No way. Not unless I was Abramovich with a few million that I didn't need.

Alan Buckley signed me as an apprentice when I was leaving Dormston School in Sedgley but within a fortnight of me arriving, Bucko had been sacked and that was my first insight into just how precarious a manager's lot can be.

Tommy Coakley gave me my League debut at Fellows Park on January 2nd 1988 in the 5-2 win against Rotherham and I remember it as if it was yesterday. I went on as a sub and hit the back of the net with my first touch of the ball, only to have the goal disallowed because Trevor Christie was offside.

As I've said elsewhere the Walsall fans can be a strange lot sometimes. Tommy was appointed when Terry Ramsden bought the club and sacking Buckley, one of the most popular managers ever at Walsall, was a decision that did not sit easily with the majority of fans. It was not Tommy's fault, but the fans hated him in his early days because this ageing little Scot with little hair and glasses was unknown in the game and had taken their hero's job.

He was known as Tommy who? and he used to come into the dressing room on matchdays covered in spit and phlegm. And that was from our own supporters!

It must be difficult trying to do a job under those circumstances but he just got on with it, never moaned and he won those same fans over when he got the club promoted thanks to victory over Bristol City in the play-offs with David Kelly scoring a hat-trick which paved the way for a big money move to West Ham.

But the club made a big mistake by selling Ned and not replacing him with an out-and-out goalscorer. We struggled to hold our own and it was inevitable that Tommy got the sack after such a wretched run of results. It was a shame really because he was an extremely likeable manager who defended his players through thick and thin.

John Barnwell pitched up next having managed Wolves and he was another of those hard-line gaffers who was never slow to offer his opinion. He absolutely slated me one day and called me all the names under the sun, but stuck me in the team at left-back. I was out of position but I must have had a good game because afterwards he put his arm around me . . . and gave me a two-and-half-year extension on my contract.

Barney always said you never have fitted carpets when you are a manager and I remember he always got to the ground at least a couple of hours early to check his stocks and shares in the Financial Times. He had a shrewd business brain and he's got a nice niche now for himself as chairman of the League Managers Association.

Most of my mates are Wolves fans and I remember playing at Molineux. During the warm-up I had seen the lads in the stand and shared a bit of banter with them about how little old Walsall were going to beat the mighty Wolves on their own muckheap and it was all good natured stuff.

That was until an incident early in the game when I accidentally caught Andy Sinton, one of their star players, and he had to go off injured. It was purely an accidental collision and anyone who knows me, knows I am not a dirty player.

71

But all of a sudden friendship turned to hatred and my mates were really giving me the verbals calling me a dirty bastard and all that. That fired me up all the more and big Andy Rammell scored the goal that gave us a 2-1 win. Boy how we enjoyed that, but it was surprising how quickly friends had turned against me and some of them still haven't forgiven me to this day.

MAVERICKS

They have been branded as rogues or mavericks, but two of the best players ever to grace the English game are also two of the nicest blokes you could wish to meet. Stan Collymore and Paul Gascoigne have more talent in their little fingers than I'll ever have but they have been vilified by the media, and unfairly so in my opinion.

Stan and I started our apprenticeship together at Walsall and right from day one you could see he was an exceptional talent. He had pace, power, brilliant skill on the ball and was good in the air - in my book the complete player and I reckon he should have been first choice striker for England. Who knows, that sort of acclaim might just have kept him on the straight and narrow a bit more.

Even in his early days as a pro Stan had problems off the field and they were to become tabloid headlines later on. I know players who have struggled with alcohol and drug abuse, gambling and other addictions and it's easy to pigeon-hole people without really understanding the cause of their problems. Stan suffered from depression which is a very complex illness requiring specialist treatment and is beyond the comprehension of most people.

People only seem to see the bad side of the man, not the intelligent, caring and generous side. Sure he could be jack the lad but then again, can't we all from time to time? I'm sure almost each and every one of us, have done something at some time we are not proud of, but it seems every tiny thing Stan does gets blown up out of all proportion.

Okay he was out of order for what he did to Ulrika Jonsson when they were an item, but few people know the full account of what happened or the level of provocation there was at the time. It happened at a World Cup party in Paris when Ulrika joined a party being thrown by some Scots supporters. They were all well on the way to being drunk and when Stan arrived, a England player, he was subjected to all manner of abuse from people who do not exactly like the English.

The upshot was that Ulrika did nothing to stop the goading. Now it takes a hell of a lot for any man to hit a woman and while I'm not condoning it in any way, you must understand that something really made him snap. There's always two sides to an argument and these were two extremely strong characters.

But in his book, and on television recently, Stan showed what an honest man he is. He candidly talked through the Ulrika incident and the "dogging" shame that was exposed in the Sun and I believe he may have won a few new admirers because of his honesty. Yes he has had a troubled past, but I wish people would stop knocking him and accept him now for the lovely, caring man he is.

Once, I had been to a PFA awards night in London and as usual, got well and truly hammered. I had sat next to the actor Ray Winstone who is one of my all-time heroes and I was like a kid in a sweet shop to be in his company. He too was like a kid in a sweet shop for a different reason because he is a genuine football fan - an Eastender who loves West Ham - and he called out players' names as he spotted them. Look, there's Teddy - that sort of thing.

As the booze flowed so my memory became more hazy and I was talking to Stan next day about the night before. I mentioned that I had seen Ray

Winstone at the do but I was disappointed because I had not had the chance to meet him.

Stan then came out with the most amazing statement: Meet him? You bloody muppet. You fell asleep on his shoulder! I could not believe it but Stan assured me it was true.

Stan had been involved in presenting a TV programme one day at the Red Cube, a well-known haunt in London of the music profession, and had called me in as a VIP guest even though I had had one or two drinks - well okay quite a few more in fact. In the VIP lounge were Jordan (aka Katie Price) and Dwight Yorke who she was seeing at the time, and also Sol Campbell. Stan was a great host and also sent over a bottle of champagne.

I went to thank him afterwards but he shrugged it off and merely told me that he never forgot his mates and knew I would enjoy myself.

Stan helped out at the opening of the restaurant I have a financial stake in and we noticed in the first few weeks that quite a lot of people were arriving saying someone had recommended us. That was Stan putting the word around for me without being asked and that's the sort of mate he is.

One of Martin O'Connor's (a Walsall team-mate) favourite stories is about Stan when they were playing together at Crystal Palace, in a reserve game against non-League opposition in a cup tie. It was the equivalent of the Birmingham Senior Cup in this part of the world. It was nothing to write home about and with the score still 0-0 and time running out, Stan asked Martin: "Is this nearly finished now? Don't tell me we've got penalties as well".

Martin's response was yes, there would be penalties, but only after 30 minutes extra time to which Stan said: "Sod that, give me the ball." And with that he went off on an amazing run, beat three defenders and lashed the ball into the top corner.

"I don't do extra time," he said. The referee blew for full-time and the Palace players were all standing there with their mouths open just wondering at Stan's ability.

Paul Gascoigne is someone else who has had more than his fair share of problems but he too is another man I admire. He is so typical of the Geordie 'work hard, play hard' culture and he has a wicked sense of humour to go with it. I've met him a few times and believe me he would do anything for you.

Richard Green, who I played alongside in my last days at Walsall, is a top bloke and I think it's fair to say he was my big boozing mate. After training at Lilleshall we would often stop off for a pint on the way home and one day we were just settling nicely into a session when he thought it best to ring his missus and warn her we were running late.

Greeny started the car up in the car park, left the engine running and rang home, telling his wife he was at a stand still. The car had not moved in 20 minutes and it looked as though there was an accident up front and no sign of movement in the near future. She could hear the traffic as he had wound down the window. True she could hear the odd car go past occasionally, but he hadn't reckoned on his wife's powers of observation because she recognised the steady tick, tick, tick of the indicator and he had been rumbled. "If you have not moved in 20 minutes, why is your indicator on - get back now!"

One of the things he taught me was that when you get home from training and you've had a pint, dive into the fridge straight away and open a can of beer before the wife can spot you. That way she can't say anything about the smell of beer on your breath.

I always followed the golden rule in football about no alcohol 48 hours before a game, but Greeny didn't. In fact I can vividly remember him picking up the sponsors man of the match award one afternoon having

76

drunk eight pints the night before.

I used to share a room with him on away trips and while he is one of the nicest blokes you can wish to meet he does have one big problem: He walks in his sleep. Many's the time I've had to steer him back into his room when he's gone walkabout in the early hours and the strange thing is he can never remember a single thing about it.

One night we were tucked up in a hotel in preparation to play Gillingham next day and I had rescued Greeny from his latest midnight stroll, got him back to bed and thought that was it for the night as I settled down to sleep.

I awoke in absolute agony because somehow Greeny had got me on my back , straddled my chest and was trying desperately to rip my nose off my face. It took all my strength to fight him off - he's a big bloke - but as soon as I did he just ambled back to bed and started snoring again, completely oblivious to the damage he had done to my hooter. And while the lads took the piss something rotten next morning at the mashed state of my nose, Greeny could only apologise and look sheepish. He still can't believe he attacked me like that.

They are some decent people in the game, but watching England's wives and girlfriends during the World Cup made me realise just what evil gold-digging bitches some women can be. I have got mates who have been fleeced of everything, so much so they would have had more left if they had fallen into a pool of piranhas..

There's one story I hear about a player who, realising his marriage was breaking down and heading for divorce, arranged to look after his wife and the two kids financially. She had the house, car, everything and it wasn't until he got into a relationship with another woman some time later that he found out he was infertile and firing blanks!

Another player always let his missus look after their money and financial affairs. He thought everything was okay, he had a good marriage and trusted her. But he too found out, too late, that she was doing the dirty on him behind his back. She had emptied the joint bank account and cleared off with another bloke before he realised anything was going on.

But the saddest, most painful parting I know of concerns a former international player who cheated on his missus just once when he was pissed and had a one night stand. He had always been the perfect husband and it was typical of his honesty that next day he sat his wife down and confessed everything to her, begging her forgiveness.

I know a lot of men would have said nothing and hoped they got away with it, but not him because he loved her so much and was so full of remorse. And he accepted his punishment when she walked out and took everything including the car. So you can imagine how he felt a couple of days later when he's standing waiting at a bus stop and his car goes past . . . with a man driving it. His missus had only been cheating on him for quite some time and had moved her fancy man in within days of their break-up.

FOREIGNERS

English football really has become cosmopolitan with the influx of so many foreign players. It was not so long ago that an average fan couldn't name a Barcelona player but now he could probably name the team and formation they play, that's how global the game has become.

Players such as Zola, Bergkamp, Henry etc have been so good for the game and set an example of how a professional sportsman should behave on and off the pitch, and even Walsall have had their share of gems over the years.

Jeff Peron was simply the best player I have played alongside and he was the catalyst that started a whole new way of thinking as the culture changed seemingly overnight. While we used to head off for a Big Mac and a couple of pints after training, Jeff would eat an apple, drink water and probably do some more training on his own. That's how they did things in France, he explained, and we thought that if that helped make him the class player he is, we ought to give it a try.

Roger Boli was another Frenchman and they were the first two players we had at Bescot who could not speak fluent English so it was a learning curve for all of us. Mind you, I'm sure Roger was conning us because he had a good knowledge of English swear words when he needed them!

But unless you're a household name coming from abroad, you are never 100 per cent sure of what you're getting. It seemed that for every 20 or so given an opportunity, only one or two would prove worth it but there again if you don't buy a ticket, you don't win the raffle.

We thought Walsall had pulled off the biggest coup of all when they landed Jean-Jacques Eydelie who had played in the 1993 European Cup final for Marseille who beat AC Milan 1-0. It was soon after that that a match-fixing and bribes scandal was exposed involving Marseille's Bernard Tapie, the club were stripped of their title and Eydelie pitched up at Bescot. An amazing sequence really.

Anyway Eydelie proved the real deal and left us breathless with his skill in a trial match and of course, Walsall snapped him up in double quick time. But in his first game for us he was a disgrace, ambled about and you could tell he couldn't be bothered.

When we had a go at him his attitude left us speechless. He more or less said: I play well, I get paid, I don't play well, I still get paid. Kerching. Well when that happens, and he's signed a contract, he's got the club by the short and curlies and there's not a fat lot you can do about it.

At Walsall we've had some great characters over the years and one of the first to make his mark was Charlie Ntamark, the laid-back Cameroon international who became a firm favourite with the fans. Sierra Leone international John Keister, nicknamed the assassin, became a dressing room legend because he suffered from monstrous piles and we've had more than our fair share of Spanish waiters and Carlos Kickaball posers.

Without doubt one of the most outrageous was Scott Ollerenshaw, an Australian winger. He was a top bloke and he went up in our estimation one day in the summer when a few of us went to see Warwickshire play Australia at Edgbaston.

Being a typically brash Aussie, he told us he knew everything there was to know about cricket and bragged that he was friends with all the superstars who regularly thrashed the Poms and were the best in the world.

As the players were leaving the field at the end of one session of play, Scotty suddenly yelled: Hey tugga ya fat bastard, how's it going? It was then we realised he was shouting to Steve Waugh, the captain of Australia and one of the best cricketers the world has ever seen. So you can imagine we were even more gobsmacked when Waugh looked up and said: Scotty. How ya doing mate? See you in the bar.

Yep, he really did know him. And that was not the only time Scott was to indulge in a spot of name dropping. He had represented Australia at the Olympics and took great delight in telling us that he came down to breakfast one day at the Olympic Village and there was just the one empty chair at the table between two 'sheilas.'

Of course he went for it, and started chatting up these two women who were amused at the shy, retiring manner of this bloke. It turned out that these sheilas played tennis and it was only Steffi Graf and Gabriela Sabatini, two of the most beautiful women in the world.

WHEN IT'S OVER

Most people think it's a great life being a professional footballer - all the money, fame and all the trappings that go with it. It can be that and it's certainly better than shovelling shit or emptying the bins.

It's not all beer and skittles though, there are the down sides such as when you suffer a major injury and you have to sit there doing nothing, just watching day-time telly, waiting until you can get back playing again. That can be really depressing.

And coming back on the coach on a freezing January night after a 0-0 draw at Darlington isn't exactly glamourous and an experience to warm the soul either.

I have a mate who is a self-made millionaire and he said to me: "Marshy, I'd give anything to play in front of a full house at Old Trafford, score against Leeds on Match of the Day and have your name plastered all over the back page. Would you swap any of it?"

The answer would be a definite no because you cannot put a price on any of that. Money simply cannot buy all the experiences I have had and if I could turn back the clock I wouldn't change a thing. Football has been good to me and let's be honest, it's most blokes' dream to play the game he loves and be paid for it. I was one of the lucky ones.

But what do you do when your career is over? That's when you face your ultimate test of character and frankly, I must admit I could have done better for myself.

I retired from playing when I was 33 and the first time it hit me was when we went on a family holiday. Having to make sure I had got my passport, packing a suitcase, finding out which gate to go to at the airport - this was all new territory for me because until then everything had been done for me and it was a real culture shock. It hits home just what a pampered life I had had, even at the lower end of the League.

There was another occasion that showed just how reliant I had become on other people doing things for me. It was at a meal for all the wives and girlfriends and being the last to leave the bar I was seated across the other side of the room from my ex-wife Louise who always looked after my food and told me what to eat. She didn't exactly make me wear a bib and spoon feed me but you get the picture.

I ordered king prawns for a starter and because she had not been there to look after me, I started to eat it. I thought it was chewy and it wasn't until I had been wrestling with this thing in my mouth for about five minutes that someone leaned over and told me you are supposed to remove the shell first. Well how was I supposed to know that?

Just what do you do with so much time on your hands when you do call it a day? Unless you are a Premiership player earning millions you will need to find work of some description. I know I did because at the level I played you cannot afford to sit on your arse doing nothing. Bills have to be paid and the pension and nest egg you put away doesn't last for ever.

There are so many hangers-on who are all over you when you're playing and if I had a penny for every time one of them said 'I'll find you a job' I'd be a rich man now and wouldn't need to work again. Funnily enough, you can never find them when you need them.

Most players of my era do not have a trade when they leave. Some stay in football as coaches or managers, some, if they're lucky enough, get into the media, but I needed to work. I put some of my savings into a courier business which did well enough for a year but wasn't making enough profit so I then invested in a sandwich shop right in the heart of the Black Country. That did okay too, especially after Steve Bull agreed to open it for me. That was quite humbling too because Bully is a legend in these parts, is Wolves' record goal scorer and like me, is a Black Country lad through and through who never forgets his roots. That's one of the reasons why he is still so popular. The other reason, of course, is he is an absolutely bostin bloke as we say in these parts.

If you had told me five years ago that I would be working in a kitchen frying black pudding for breakfast I'd say you were having a laugh. But the shop did well, I sold it and made a few quid and I've got a few fingers in various business interests now including a restaurant in Walsall town centre - but I know I'm never going to be a millionaire unless my six numbers come up on Saturday night.

The point is I have always been prepared to work hard to earn a crust. I know one particular player who started at the bottom, got lucky, moved up into the Premiership and even got into the England side. But his attitude is like 'I don't give a toss - I'm set up for life now' and he's a vastly different character altogether. Money has gone to his head and he's not the same likeable person he used to be.

I always admired Mike Tyson as a boxer. I recently saw him on telly and he was in Las Vegas sparring. People were paying to watch him train, as he struggles to pay off his debts reported to be $250million. I thought then what a sad, forlorn figure he looked. It reminded me of someone in football who had been surrounded by hangers-on but once his career was over, that's it. No-one wants to know any more.

Even in football there are the haves and have-nots and I must admit there are times when I've scratched my head wondering just whether the PFA could help its members more. Recently there was a very high profile case where a Premiership player was named and shamed in a Sunday tabloid over some seedy affair. I'm not going to go into the specifics for obvious reasons but the point is the PFA coughed up £100,000 to help him in his defence.

Contrast that to a player from the bottom division who finds his wages are not big enough to cover his outgoings. The PFA benevolent fund will pay a maximum of £6,000 to help pay his bills and I just don't think it's fair. It's lopsided and loaded in favour of the big name players.

Another thing that really annoyed me was the whole Rio Ferdinand drugs test affair and the way it was handled. Now people may not be aware of this, but when FA testing officers call in at your club all the players' names are put in a hat and some are selected at random. I know, having been picked out more than once, that when your name is called there is no way on earth you can escape without providing a sample.

The testing man is virtually joined to you at the hip from that moment you are picked out. No matter if you go in for a shower, to your car, have a drink, that bloke is there with you all the time and he'll go home with you if necessary and wait until the early hours just as long as he gets his urine sample.

Now I don't want to get into the whys and wherefores of Rio's case and I'm not suggesting for one minute that he had something to hide. All I am questioning is the difference there appears to be in the treatment of lower league players in contrast to their Premiership colleagues. In my experience, it was impossible not to give a sample when requested, and maybe, if the FA testing people treated premiership players in the same way, Rio wouldn't have been able to avoid giving a sample and would not have had to face the subsequent fine and ban that was imposed.

Having said that there are some genuine nice guys at the top who don't forget their roots. We were playing at Blackburn one day and typical

Marshy I was first to the bar afterwards to get a round in. What I hadn't reckoned with was Premiership prices! The £15 I had in my grubby little paw was nowhere near enough because the round came to well over £30 which meant a whip-round amongst the lads.

We were scraping together the odd quid here and 50p there, loads of shrapnel and all looking very sheepish and embarrassed. Then Ashley Ward wandered over and said "here lads, let me help you" and bunged in enough cash to more than make up the difference.

But he did it in such as way that he wasn't being a flash git and there was not a hint of arrogance, just a recognition of the fact that he could help out some fellow pros who were not as well paid as him. Of course there were one or two comments flying about and some people did take the piss, but they were laughing with us rather than at us and in fact Ashley was grinning when he asked if we could afford chips for the coach journey home. I though that was a nice, humble touch from a player who had worked his way up the ladder.

Goodbye Matt

I hope that I have given you some fun and raised a few smiles with just some of the antics that I was able to print, but there is a serious side to me and I would like to send a message to all young players starting out in the game.

Football is a wonderful way of making a living and if you do it right, get your head down, work hard, stay off the booze and really apply yourself you can retire a rich man. Then you can clown about and get pissed as much as you like, but don't follow my example and do things the wrong way round.

You only get one shot at life so please, try and do things right and enjoy every minute of it because you never know what's around the corner. An injury could finish your career in an instant so make sure you look after yourself.

And I make no apologies for ending my book with a personal tribute to Matt Gadsby who was so cruelly taken from us just after his 27th birthday. Matt started his career at Walsall and I can put my hand on my heart and say he was one of the most popular players I have ever met anywhere. I cannot think of anyone who has ever had a bad word to say about him.

He collapsed and died while playing for Hinckley and I'm sure he would have liked to go that way, doing something he loved. But 27 is no age and it's only when you come across tragedies like this that you stop and think where your life is heading.

There was a tremendous turnout for his funeral with not a dry eye in the church and it was interesting to see the different characters who had gathered from the clubs he had played for. Without naming names there was someone driving a Bentley who had played for England, Premiership players, some who had earned a good living when they left the pro game and some, like myself, who are scratching out a living and getting by. There was also someone on special release from prison and someone who is bankrupt. A right mixed bunch.

I could not help contrast that with the Chelsea players who went to see their goalkeeper Petr Cech when he ended up in hospital recently as the result of an accidental collision during their match against Reading. There were big, expensive cars all over the place and there was such an obvious difference between Premiership millionaires and lower division journeymen and that is the point I'm trying to make to the kids of today. If you want it, it's there for you.

Darryl Burgess is a good mate and I will never forget something he said about me when we were at Northampton. He told a mutual acquaintance: Marshy is one of the nicest blokes I've ever met. If someone told me in five years time that he was dead it would break my heart . . . . but I would not be surprised.

Just like Matt's sad, untimely death, it's a sobering thought. God bless you, mate.

What others say about Chris

I was asked recently if I could say a few words about Marshy or tell a story from our playing days for his new book. I could tell many a story, but I thought Sod it, there is no story I could tell that Marshy wouldn't have mentioned in this book already. So I thought I would write a small passage sucking up to his big hairy arse, but then I also thought no.

All you need to know about Marshy is that he is one of the nicest, most genuine people that you could ever wish to meet and the best full back I have ever had the pleasure to play with in my career.

All those of you that know Marshy don't need me to tell you about him. It's been a pleasure Mendip!

DARREN WRACK (WALSALL TEAM-MATE)

Chris Marsh is a friend that would do anything for you. Over the years since we have both left Walsall, he is one of the people who has always kept in touch, given me a ring to see how things are going. I would count him as a good mate, and unfortunately, although I would like to, I can't think of anything bad to say about him.

On my first day at Walsall I first encountered Marshy and he walked right past me and blanked me which was a friendly welcome - but found out since

91

that despite my first impression, he is a top man, and we became firm friends. One story I remember, we were playing Preston away and Marshy, being the ultimate professional forgot his boots. Fortunately I had a spare pair that fit, and my influence obviously worked as he scored an absolute screamer of a goal - almost as good as the one I scored that day! He did try to buy those boots from me for the next week but I was hanging onto them.

MARTIN O'CONNER ("SKIP" - FORMER WALSALL CAPTAIN)

Marshy the player - the saying "Jack of all trades, master of none" doesn't apply to Marshy; he mastered most positions during his career although I would suggest his best position was full-back. He is well known for his "Step-over", not because it was a good trick - but because it was his only trick!

Marshy the person - he was an institution at Walsall. He was at the centre of anything arranged socially and many of the pranks that occurred - and Walsall had a good "drinking team" at the time. As a team we did go out drinking - but only on the days we were supposed to, and I think the fans realised that. We didn't mind having a drink in Walsall, usually on a Wednesday or Saturday after a game. We had a great affinity with the fans - especially Marshy. They weren't shy in telling us if we had played crap - but they always knew we had done our best.

It's a pleasure and a privilege to know and have played with Chris.

STUART WATKISS (FORMER WALSALL TEAM-MATE)

Marshy is a Top Man in my book and a great friend. You could always rely on him on the pitch - and you can always rely on him off the pitch. Last Man Standing - he always had a pint in his hand, and could match anyone I have ever met drink for drink - despite what size glass the other person is holding or whatever was in it! If Jackie Wilson or Armand Van Heldan comes on and you are in his company, you are likely to see him strutting his stuff.

I can't speak highly enough of Chris as a mate, we have been friends for a long time and you can always rely on him.

DARRYL BURGESS (FORMER NORTHAMPTON TEAM-MATE)

Without a doubt the biggest character we've ever met in football! and an absolute legend of it, but to start with the football. What Marshy has done in football cannot be questioned, what is it 500 games? Not bad for a fat lad from Dudley who played on the wing but had no pace, bad touch, couldn't cross and didn't really score a lot of goals that is some achievement!

But on a serious note the king of the step over was a top player and underrated by many Walsall Fans and some Managers but never by the players. In the dressing room Marshy was top man, and as for off the pitch Mad Dog was in a league of his own. There are just to many stories to mention, that could be a book of it's own, if it was allowed to be printed, but we will leave you with our favourite story of Mad Dog, On a end of season trip in Tenerife. We were all out in a Bar and Mad Dog was buying drinks for everyone. After ordering every round of drinks and paying he proceeded to throw his change over his shoulder on to the floor telling any one who would listen that he was a legend and that he could afford it. Later that evening at approx 4:00 am we both noticed some-body crawling around the floor in the bar and to our horror it was Mad Dog. When we asked him if he was alright he asked us if we could lend him some money so he could buy a drink as he had thrown his money away. To finish we would like to say Thank You, you were always there to look after us in our years together and really took us under your wing !

CLIVE PLATT AND WAYNE THOMAS,
(YOUNGSTERS CHRIS HELPED SETTLE IN AT WALSALL)

As a player, Chris was one of the most consistent players at the level at which he played. He was highly regarded by the fans at Walsall during the time he was there and was probably one of the most consistent names on the team sheet. He was a great guy to have in the team as a captain, because he didn't rock any boats, or cause any tension, he was just always out to do his best, week-in and week-out.

As a Scotsman, he took the pressure off me, as he was probably the only person tighter than me in the dressing room. Most of the stories I could tell are un-printable, but the one constant was that any night out with Marshy involved - was a good night out.

Even though I would like to stitch him up - all I can honestly say is he would never let you down and is a truly likeable guy, although I think the title of the book should have been The Good, the Bad and the Ugly!

TOM BENNETT (FORMER WALSALL TEAM-MATE)

Chris Marsh as a player was outstanding at the level he played at, and, but for unfortunate injuries could probably have played at an even higher level than he achieved with Walsall. He always had a good touch on the ball, was brave in the tackle and even got a few goals too.

He was great to have in the dressing room and always had a joke to share and was enthusiastic about Walsall. He always had loads of stories to tell of his previous managers and players to those of us that joined the club whilst he was there.

The year I spent at Walsall was probably one of the best I have had for camaraderie in the dressing room and Chris had a lot to do with that team spirit.

MARK ROBBINS (EX-MANCHESTER UNITED AND FORMER WALSALL TEAM-MATE)

Marshy was a great player, people talk about how good Ronaldo's step-over is, but Walsall fans know that Marshy's was much better! The roar he used to get from the crowd each time he did it was great.

Marshy was a real "team man". One year on a club trip there was a "hanger-on" that we didn't really want on the trip - not one of the players, and we didn't really want him there. So Marshy and I gave the guy a warm welcome and threw this chap in the pool fully clothed, then a bit later saw him again so Marshy decided to throw a sausage at him - that seemed to do the trick (you had to be there really)!

Chris is also known for his drinking antics - I have even seen him drink a pint whilst doing a headstand, proving just how athletic he was!

Chris joined the club as a youngster when I was one of the older players - but he was accepted very quickly into the fold and we took him under our wing - I showed him how to drink, but warned him not to copy what I did on the pitch!

Football has changed dramatically in recent times, and the drinking culture that we had has now gone - probably for the better, but we had some really good times and tried to stick to days when it wouldn't affect our game.

MARK REES (FORMER WALSALL TEAM-MATE)

I joined Walsall as a youngster, and Chris was always a bit of a father figure to me, and looked after me. If I was ever having a bad time of it, he always told me about something that had happened to him which made things seem better, his were always worse!

He is a brilliant lad, and we have always kept in touch over the years, and I would do anything for him. His off the field antics are legendary, and he regularly got me into trouble - but he is always fun to be around.

MARTIN BUTLER (WALSALL STRIKER)

Chris Marsh - a real likeable character and an excellent player who perhaps didn't fulfil his true potential, missing out on a few "big moves" for one reason or another. As player coach, it was nice to have such a versatile player to choose. He played at full back, either left or right and on either wing, and excelled wherever you asked him to play.

Marshy was always a great guy to have in the changing rooms, he was everyone's friend and always had a great laugh. There aren't many players who play for a club as long as Chris did, and he was rewarded with his testimonial season, and he really deserved it. That kind of thing rarely happens in football - especially the higher up the divisions you look.

KEVIN WILSON,

(EX-PLAYER-COACH AT WALSALL AND NORTHAMPTON

TOWN MANAGER)

Top-man - that's Marsh., I started as a youngster whilst Chris was there, and he always looked out for the younger players - and we are still great friends now.

As I say - he looked out for us, but one story I remember was when we were staying at a hotel in Luton, before flying out on a trip abroad - I was only about 19, and he was one of the more senior team members. Instead of him looking out for me that time, it was me who had to pick up a collapsed Marshy who was flat out on the floor and get him undressed and into his bed when he returned to the hotel drunk.

I cannot speak highly enough of Marshy, he was Top-man in the dressing room and is still a good mate now.

DEAN KEATES (WALSALL TEAM-MATE)

Marshy as I'm sure others have mentioned has a great sense of humour. One particular memory of mine was his tendency to try to convince us that he was Italian. On one trip to Ayia Napa, for 3 or 4 days he only spoke in Italian - which was quite funny as he only had about 3 words in his vocabulary. As a team-mate he was always good to have on the pitch - but in the changing rooms and on social nights he was a pleasure to have around.

ADRIAN VIVEASH (FORMER WALSALL TEAM-MATE)

When Walsall people speak of Chris Marsh, two thoughts immediately spring to mind, one, he will be a Walsall F.C hero for all of his days, he is a Saddler through and through and two, there are not many like him around in professional football.

Chris's game was built on immense power, an unbelievable will to win, a great engine, a willingness to play anywhere on the park and the greatest 'step over' in professional football.

I've known 'Marshy' since his apprentice days at Walsall, when the senior pro's and I would go for a night out, Chris was always included, unusual for an apprentice, but he always had a solid character and will always be 'one of the boys'.

I saw his debut, when coming on as a substitute. He scored after seven seconds, which would have been a league record but was unfortunately disallowed, as one of our players was slow coming out and caught offside. With today's offside rule the goal would have stood.

'Marshy' went on to be in the top ten of all time appearance makers for Walsall. He played in every position on the park, one week it could be right back, the next outside left, and when our keeper got injured, 'Marshy' was the first one with his hand up, a job he did a couple of times. So Walsall fans took him to their heart, he was and is, one of us. I firmly believe had he been a little more selfish and insisted on playing

97

in one position either right back or right side of midfield, at his best, he could have landed the big move. There's always speculation and rumours in football, but at one time we all knew that a couple of Premiership clubs as they are known now, were taking a look, including Liverpool for a short time. That was not to be, but it shows how close Chris got to the big time.

The most joyous moments of Chris's Walsall career for me, was the goal against Oldham at The Bescot on May 1st 1999, it was the moment we all knew we were going into The Championship and it was right that it was 'Marshy's' moment. The other, the opening goal against Leeds United in the FA Cup on December 4th 1994, that forced a replay.
Only three days earlier Chris had been with me at the NEC to meet R.Kelly one of my artists who was on tour, on the Monday after the match, R.Kelly had been watching TV in a hotel room and asked me, you know that footballer I met, I saw someone on TV who looked like him scoring a goal. Yes, Robert, that is the legend they call 'Marshy'.

Much will be written about Chris and his passion for a good night out and a good drink, I've experienced a few nights with him, but one should always remember it takes great determination to have a full career in professional football and I've known Chris go through a few season's 'dry', when he felt his game was not right.

For me, 'Marshy' makes the All Time Walsall FC eleven, he's been one of my best mates for years and has supported me through all the good and bad times in my music career. He is and always will be a hero, and if Ronaldo of Manchester United wants to learn how to do the 'Step over' properly, he best give Chris a call.

Good Luck with the book and life.

STEVE JENKINS,
MANAGING DIRECTOR OF JIVE RECORDS 1989-2004
AND A SADDLER.